Alan Dunn's
CHRISTMAS CAKES

NEW HOLLAND

Published in 2010 by New Holland Publishers (UK) Ltd
London • Cape Town • Sydney • Auckland
www.newhollandpublishers.com

Garfield House
86-88 Edgware Road
London W2 2EA
United Kingdom

80 McKenzie Street
Cape Town 8001
South Africa

Unit 1, 66 Gibbes Street
Chatswood, NSW 2067
Australia

218 Lake Road
Northcote, Auckland
New Zealand

10 9 8 7 6 5 4 3 2 1

A catalogue record for this book is available from the British Library

ISBN 978 1 84773 771 7

Senior Editor: Corinne Masciocchi
Designer: Peter Crump
Photographer: Sue Atkinson
Production Controller: Laurence Poos
Editorial Director: Rosemary Wilkinson

Reproduction by PDQ Digital Media Solutions Ltd, United Kingdom
Printed and bound by Times Offset (M) Sdn Bhd, Malaysia

Dedicated and thank you to Alice Christie, Norma Laver, Sathyavathi Narayanswami, Sue Atkinson, Jenny Walker, Tombi Peck, Andrew Lockey, John Quoi Hoi, Tony Warren, Beverley Dutton, Sue Hodges, Doreen Macmurdie, Christine Giles, Avril and Allen Dunn, Susan Laird, and finally, to the memory of my grandfather, Ernie Blair.

CONTENTS

Introduction

There is something very special about baking and decorating a Christmas cake, although it can be a rather daunting process, especially when there are so many other things to organize and think of at this often frantic time of year.

I was 14 when my grandfather Blair, a baker, taught me how to make my very first Christmas cake. As much as I enjoyed baking the cake, what I was really looking forward to doing was decorating it. This involved a great deal of research and gathering as many books on cake decorating as I could lay my hands on. The local library was a good source, and the cake that took my fancy was royal iced with partial peaks and gold dragées, with a rice paper picture of a red robin. But the cake I attempted to recreate was awful and the icing set so hard that an electric carving knife was needed to cut into it! However, it was my first proper attempt at decorating a cake and the start of a lifelong passion. Gradually, and with a lot of practice, my work improved and my parents and grandparents were amazed and very supportive of my progress.

I have a real passion for decorating Christmas cakes, so when New Holland asked me to write this book, I did not hesitate to accept. To get me into the Christmas mood, I put up my Christmas tree and decorations far earlier than usual – which meant that my cats had a prolonged period of playing with baubles and generally causing mischief while I carried on regardless! I am indebted to my friend Sathya, whose house I completely took over while creating and finishing most of the cakes for this book. It is the longest Christmas any of us has ever had, ending at the start of February, when the photo shoots were finally over!

Most of the cake designs featured are floral-themed, which is my own personal taste and area of particular interest, but there are also several simpler designs that require no flowers and that are great fun to create when time is short.

The baubles and decorations are now all safely put away, but I find myself excited at the prospect of this book being published for Christmas, when it will be time to start the wonderful crazy process all over again! So, Merry Christmas to you all and I hope you experience as much pleasure decorating your Christmas cakes as I do!

Alan Dunn

Equipment and materials

Cake and sugar floral designs can be achieved using a small selection of cake decorating tools, however, you will find that many of the items listed here will save you time which is especially important during the lead up to Christmas when time is often very short!

Equipment

Non-stick board This is an essential addition to the flowermaker's work box. Avoid white boards as they strain the eyes too much. Some boards can be very shiny, making it difficult to frill the petals against them. If this is the case, simply roughen up the surface using some fine glass paper prior to use or turn over the board and use the back, which is often less shiny. I always apply a thin layer of white vegetable fat rubbed into the surface of the board, then remove most of the excess with dry kitchen paper – this stops the paste sticking to the board and also makes you check each time to see if it is clean from food colour. Be careful when washing the board – if the water is too hot it will cause the board to warp.

Rolling pins It's good to have a selection of non-stick rolling pins in various sizes. They are essential for rolling out flowerpaste, sugarpaste and almond paste successfully.

Foam pads Foam pads are ideal to place petals and leaves on while you soften the edges – especially if you have hot hands that tend to dissolve the petals as you are working them. Prior to buying this product, check that it has a good surface as some have a rough-textured surface that will tear the edges of your petals or leave marks on them. I either prefer the large blue pad called a Billy's block or the yellow celpad.

Wires and floristry tape I buy mostly white paper-covered wires, preferring to colour or tape over them as I work. The quality varies between brands. The most consistent in quality are the Japanese Sunrise wires. These are available from 35-gauge (very fine but rare) to 18-gauge (thicker). Floristry tape is used in the construction of stems and bouquets. They contain a glue that is released when the tape is stretched. I use mainly nile green, brown and white tape from the Lion Brand tape company.

Tape shredder This tool contains three razor blades to cut floristry tape into quarter widths. I have a couple of tape shredders and have removed two blades from one of them so that it cuts the tape into half widths. It is often best to use a tiny amount of cold cream rubbed onto the blades with a cotton bud and also a little onto the lid that presses against the blades to help the tape run smoothly against the blades, as it can often stick to an excess of glue left behind from the tape. It is also wise to remove any excess build-up of glue from the blades using fine-nose pliers and also to replace the blades regularly. Handle with care at all times.

Paintbrushes and dusting brushes Good-quality, synthetic brushes or synthetic-blend brushes from art shops are best for flower-making. I use mainly short, flat, not too soft bristle brushes for applying layers of food colour dusts to flowers and leaves. It is best to keep brushes for certain colours so that it takes away the need to wash them quite so regularly. I use finer sable or synthetic-blend brushes for painting fine lines or detail spots onto petals. My favourites are the yellow-handled brushes made by Daler-Rowney (system 3).

Petal, flower and leaf cutters and veiners There is a huge selection of petal, flower and leaf cutters available from cake decorating shops, both in metal and plastic. For Christmas, there are some wonderful snowflake cutters, Christmas trees, robins, reindeer, holly, poinsettia and Christmas rose cutters. Petal and leaf moulds/veiners are made from food-grade silicone rubber. They are very useful for creating natural petal and leaf texturing for sugar work. The moulds have been made using mostly real plant material, giving the finished sugar flower a realistic finish. Like the flower cutters, there is an impressive selection of commercial veiners to choose from.

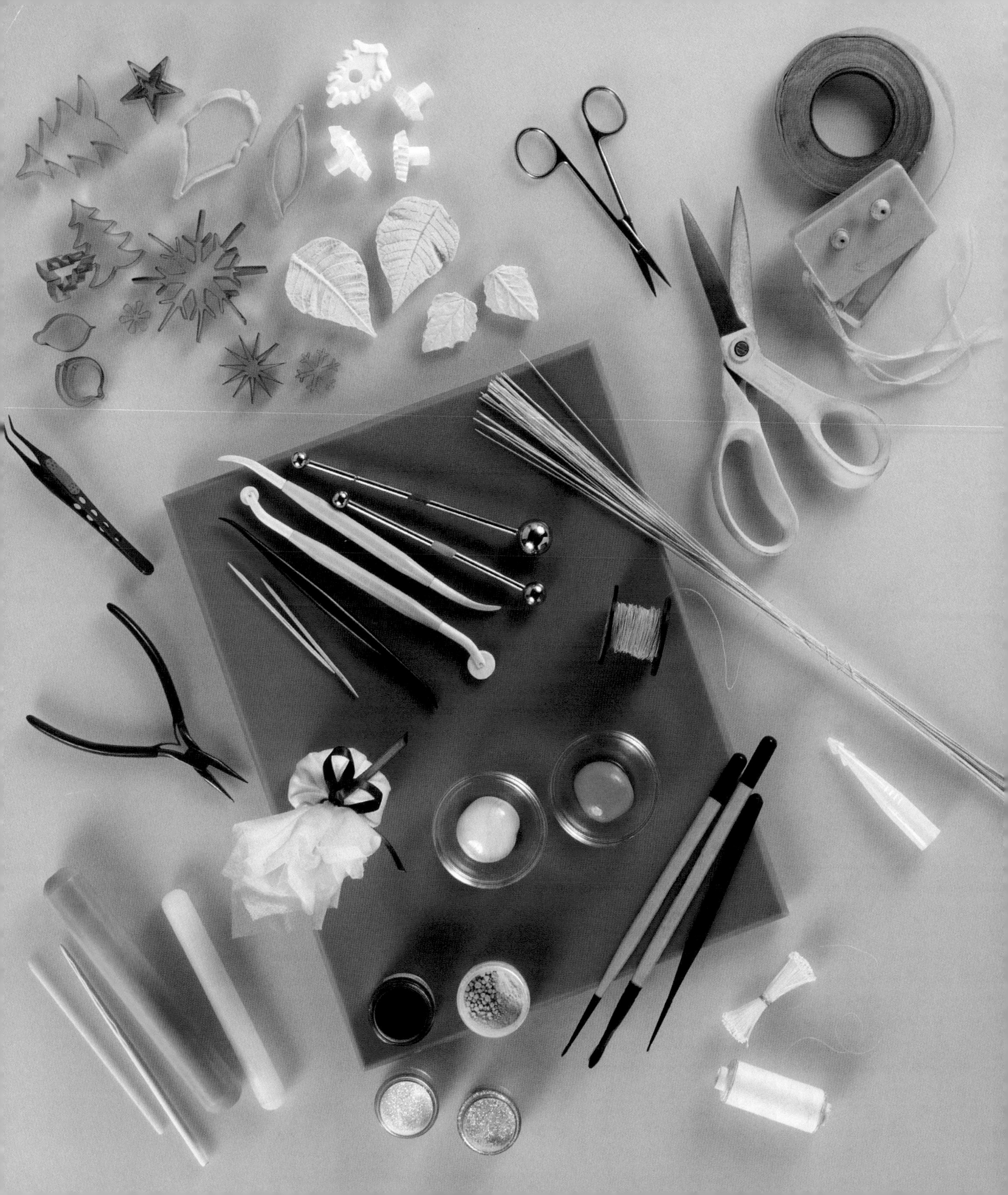

Posy picks These are made from food-grade plastic and come in various sizes. They are used to hold the handle of a spray or bouquet of flowers into the cake. The food-grade plastic protects the cake of contamination from the wires and floristry tape used in the construction of floral sprays. Never push wires directly into a cake.

Stamens and thread There is a huge selection of commercial stamens available from cake decorating shops. I use mainly fine white and seed-head stamens, which I can then colour using powder colours. Fine cotton thread is best for stamens. I use lace-making Brock 120 white thread, although some thicker threads may also be useful for larger flowers. An emery board is great for fluffing up the tips of the thread to form anthers.

Glue Non-toxic glue sticks can be bought from stationery or art shops and are great for fixing ribbon to the cake drum's edge. Always make sure that the glue does not come into direct contact with the cake. I use a hi-tack non-toxic craft glue to attach stamens to the end of wires. I feel that no harm is being done sticking inedible items together with other inedible items. However, the glue should not come into direct contact with the sugar petals as it will dissolve them.

Scissors, pliers and wire cutters Fine embroidery and curved scissors are very useful for cutting fine petals, thread and ribbons too. Larger florist's scissors are useful for cutting wires and ribbon. Small, fine-nose pliers are another essential. Good-quality pliers from electrical supply shops are best – they are expensive but well worth the investment. Electrical wire cutters are useful for cutting heavier wires.

Plain-edge cutting wheel (PME) and scalpel The plain-edge cutting wheel is rather like a small double-sided pizza wheel. It is great for cutting out quick petals and leaves, and also for adding division lines to buds. A scalpel is essential for marking veins, adding texture and cutting out petal shapes too.
Tweezers It is important to use fine, angled tweezers without ridges (or teeth). They are useful for pinching ridges on petals and holding very fine petals and stamens. They are also very handy when arranging flowers to push smaller items into difficult, tight areas of an arrangement or spray.

Metal ball tools (CC/Celcakes) I use mostly metal ball tools to work the edges of petals and leaves. These are heavier than plastic ball tools, which means that less effort is needed to soften the paste. I mostly work the tool using a rubbing or rolling action against the paste, positioning it half on the petal/leaf edge and half on my hand or foam pad the petal is resting against. It can also be used to 'cup' or hollow out petals to form interesting shapes.

Dresden/veining tool (Jem or PME) The fine end of this tool is great for adding central veins to petals or leaves, and the broader end can be used for working the edges of a leaf to give a serrated effect or a 'double-frilled' effect on the edges of petals. Simply press the tool against the paste repeatedly to create a tight, frilled effect or pull the tool against the paste on a non-stick board to create serrations. The fine end of the tool can also be used to cut into the edge of the paste to cut and flick finer serrated-edged leaves. I use a black tool by Jem for finer, smaller leaves and flowers, and the larger yellow PME tool for larger flowers.

Ceramic tools (HP/Holly Products) A smooth ceramic tool is used for curling the edges of petals and hollowing out throats of small flowers, as well as serving the purpose of a mini rolling pin. Another of the ceramic tools, known as the silk veining tool, is wonderful for creating delicate veins and frills to petal edges.

Celsticks (CC/Celcakes) Celsticks come in four sizes and are ideal for rolling out small petals and leaves and to create thick ridges. The pointed end of the tool is great for opening up the centre of 'hat'-type flowers. The rounded end can be used in the same way as a ball tool, to soften edges and hollow out petals.

Kitchen paper ring formers These are great for holding and supporting petals to create a cupped shape as they dry allowing the paste/petal to breathe, which speeds up the drying process (plastic formers tend to slow down the drying process). To make, cut a strip of kitchen paper, twist it back onto itself and then tie it in a loop, or for larger petals, cut a sheet of kitchen paper diagonally across, twist and tie.

Homemade leaf/petal veiners

There are several craft products available that can be used to make moulds for leaves, petals, fruit, nuts, etc... It is important to try to find a food-grade product. Silicone plastique is a good medium to use with a quick-drying time. When making a mould of a petal or leaf it is important to choose items with prominent veins. Note that most flowers and foliage produce stronger veins as they age. To make a mould follow the three simple steps below:

1 Silicone plastique can be purchased as a kit. Mix the two compounds together thoroughly. The white material is the base and the blue is the catalyst – once mixed you will have about 10 to 20 minutes' working time before the mixed medium sets – this often depends on the room temperature at the time. Flatten the product onto a sheet of plastic wrap or a plastic food bag: this is important as the product tends to stick to everything in its sight!

2 Press the back of your chosen leaf or petal into the silicone putty, taking care to press the surface evenly to avoid air bubbles, which will create a fault in the veiner. When the compound has set, simply peel off the leaf or petal. Trim away any excess silicone from around the mould using a pair of scissors.

3 Next, very lightly grease the leaf veiner with cold cream cleanser – be careful not to block up the veins with the cream as this will spoil the final result. Mix up another amount of the two compounds and press firmly on top of the first half of the leaf veiner, again taking care to press evenly. When the second half has set, pull the two sides apart: you now have a double-sided leaf veiner!

Materials

Egg white You will need fresh egg white to stick petals together and to sometimes alter the consistency of the paste if it is too dry. Many cake decorators avoid the use of fresh egg white because of salmonella scares. I continue to use Lion brand eggs and always work with a fresh egg white each time I make flowers. There are commercially available edible glues which can be used instead of egg white but I find that these tend to dissolve the sugar slightly before allowing it to dry, resulting in weak petals.

White vegetable fat I use this to grease non-stick boards and then wipe it off with dry kitchen paper. This does two things: it conditions the board, helping prevent the flowerpaste sticking to it, and it also removes excess food colour that might have been left from the previous flower-making session. You can also add a tiny amount of white fat to the paste if it is very sticky, however, take care not to add too much as it will make the paste short and slow down the drying process. You must also be careful not to leave too much fat on the board, as greasy patches will show up on the petals when you apply the dry dusting colours.

Cornflour bag An essential if you have hot hands like mine! Cornflour is a lifesaver when the flowerpaste is sticky. It is best to make a cornflour bag using disposable nappy liners; these can be bought from most large chemists. Fold a couple of layers of nappy liners together and add a good tablespoon of cornflour on top. Tie the nappy liner together into a bag using ribbon or an elastic band. This bag is then used to lightly dust the paste prior to rolling it out and also on petals/leaves before they are placed into a veiner.

Petal dusts These are my favourite forms of food colour. These food colour dusts contain a gum which helps them to adhere to the petal or leaf. They are wonderful for creating very soft and also very intense colouring to finished flowers. The dusts can be mixed together to form different colours or brushed on in layers which I find creates more interest and depth to the finished flower or leaf. White petal dust can be added to soften the colours (some cake decorators add cornflour but I find this weakens the gum content of the dust, often causing a streaky effect to the petal). If you are trying to create bold, strong colours, it is best to dust the surface of the flowerpaste while it is still fairly pliable or at the leather-hard stage. A paint can also be made by adding clear alcohol (isopropyl) to the dust. This is good for adding spots and finer details. Another of my favourite uses of this dust is to add it to melted cocoa butter to make a paint that is ideal for painting designs onto the surface of a cake. Petal dusts can be used in small amounts to colour flowerpaste to create interesting and subtle base colours.

Paste food colours I use only a small selection of paste food colours. I prefer to work with a white or a very pale base colour and then create stronger finished colours using powder food colours. I add paste food colours into sugarpaste to cover the cakes but even then I am not a huge fan of strongly coloured cake coverings. It is best to mix up a small ball of sugarpaste with some paste food colour and then add this ball to the larger amount of paste – this will avoid you adding too much colour to the entire amount of sugarpaste. There's nothing worse than a screaming yellow cake!

Liquid colours These are generally used to colour royal icing as they alter the consistency of flowerpaste, sugarpaste and almond paste but they can also be great to paint with. I use a small selection of liquid colours to paint fine spots and fine lines to petals. I mostly use cyclamen and poinsettia red liquid colours for flower-making.

Craft dusts These are inedible and only intended for items that are not going to be eaten. Craft dusts are much stronger and much more light-fast than food colour dusts. Care must be taken as they do tend to migrate the moment you take the lid off the pot. Dust in an enclosed space as once these colours get into the air they have a habit of landing where you don't want them to! To prevent spotty cakes, it is best to keep the cake in a box while you are dusting the flowers, whether it is with these or petal dusts. Some of the craft dusts were originally food colours but because of the EEC food regulations these have been re-labelled craft dusts and are only suitable in very small diluted amounts or on items, such as sugar flowers, that are to be removed from the cake prior to cutting and eating.

Edible glaze spray There are several ways to glaze leaves. Recently I have been using an edible spray varnish made by Fabilo. This glaze can be used lightly for most leaves or sprayed in layers for shiny leaves and berries. Spray in a well-ventilated area, perhaps wearing a filter mask. Spraying leaves is much quicker than the method below which I also use from time to time.

Confectioner's varnish Confectioner's varnish can be used neat to create a high glaze on berries and foliage. I mostly dilute the glaze with isopropyl alcohol (often sold as dipping solution or glaze cleaner in cake decorating shops). This lessens the shine, giving a more natural effect for most foliage and some petals. I mix the two liquids together in a clean jam jar with a lid. Do not shake as this produces air bubbles. Leaves can be dipped straight into the glaze, shaking off the excess before hanging to dry or placing onto kitchen paper to blot off any excess. The glaze can also be painted onto the leaf but I find the bristles of the brush pull off some of the dust colour, producing a streaky effect. You need to watch the leaves, as a build-up of glaze can give a streaky shiny finish which is not desirable. I use various strengths of glaze:

- **¾ glaze** (1 part isopropyl alcohol to 3 parts confectioner's varnish). Gives a high glaze but takes away the very plastic finish often left by full, undiluted confectioner's varnish.

- **½ glaze** (equal proportions of the two). This is used to give a natural shine for many types of foliage, including ivy and rose leaves.

- **¼ glaze** (3 parts isopropyl alcohol to 1 part confectioner's varnish). This is used for leaves and sometimes petals that don't require a shine but just need something stronger than just steaming to set the colour and remove the dusty finish.

When the varnish has dried, you might like to use a scalpel to scratch or etch through the glaze into the surface of the flowerpaste to create fine white veins on the likes of ivy leaves.

Recipes

These recipes will help you along your way with the projects in this book. There are recipes for modelling pastes, royal icing and two wonderful fruitcakes too. I always buy commercial sugarpaste and almond paste so no recipes are listed for these pastes.

Fruitcake

This is my version of a recipe given to me by my friend and sugar goddess Tombi Peck! Double the quantities for a three-tier wedding cake and line another small tin just in case there is some cake mixture left over. This recipe will fill a 30 cm (12 in) round cake tin, plus a little extra for a smaller cake. Even if I only need a 20 cm (8 in) oval cake, I still make up this full quantity and bake extra cakes with the remaining mixture – it is hardly worth turning the oven on for one small cake. The variety and amount of each dried fruit can be changed to suit your own taste – not everyone is a fan of the texture of dried figs, so these can be replaced by any combination of other fruits. In the original recipe, Tombi used currants.

Ingredients

1 kg (2 lb 3 oz/8 cups) raisins
1 kg (2 lb 3 oz/8 cups) sultanas
500 g (1 lb 2 oz/4 cups) dried figs, chopped
500 g (1 lb 2 oz/4 cups) prunes, chopped
250 g (9 oz/2 cups) natural colour glacé cherries, halved
125 g (4½ oz/1 cup) dried apricots, chopped
125 g (4½ oz/1 cup) dried or glacé pineapple, chopped
Grated zest and juice of 1 orange
200 ml (7 fl oz/½ cup) brandy (the odd dash of Cointreau or cherry brandy can be good too)
500 g (1 lb 2 oz/2 cups) unsalted butter, at room temperature
250 g (9 oz/2 cups) light muscovado sugar
250 g (9 oz/2 cups) dark muscovado sugar
4 tsp apricot jam
8 tsp golden syrup
1 tsp each of ground ginger, allspice, nutmeg, cloves and cinnamon
½ tsp mace
500 g (1 lb 2 oz/4 cups) plain flour
250 g (9 oz/1½ cups) ground almonds
10 large free-range eggs, at room temperature

Use a large pair of scissors to halve and chop the various fruit that require it from the list. Add or subtract the fruit accordingly to suit your taste, but make sure the overall weight remains the same. Mix the dried fruit, orange zest and juice, and alcohol together in a plastic container with a lid. Seal the container and leave to soak for about a week if time allows. Otherwise overnight will do.

Preheat the oven to 140°C/275°F/gas 1. Cream the butter in a large bowl until soft. Gradually add the two types of sugar and beat them together. Stir in the apricot jam, golden syrup and spices (including the mace).

Sieve the flour into a separate bowl and stir in the almonds.

Beat the eggs together and add slowly to the butter/sugar mixture, alternating it with the flour/almond mix. Do not add the eggs too quickly as the mixture may curdle.

Before you add the fruit, set aside a small amount of un-fruited batter – this will be used on top of the fruited batter to stop the fruit catching on the top in the oven. Mix the soaked fruit into the remaining larger amount of batter. Grease and line the tin(s) with non-stick parchment paper. Fill the tin with batter to the required depth – I usually aim for about two-thirds the depth of the tin. Apply a thin layer of the un-fruited batter on top and smooth over. Bake for 4 to 6 hours, depending on the size of the cake and the type of oven as some cook faster than others. It is important to smell when the cake is ready. The cake should shrink slightly from the sides of the tin, be firm to the touch and smell wonderful. If in doubt test with a skewer - if it comes out clean the cake is ready.

Allow the cake to cool slightly in the tin, add a couple of extra dashes of alcohol, and leave to cool further in the tin. Store wrapped in non-stick parchment paper and plastic wrap. Allow to mature for as long as you have - a few days to a few months works well.

Royal icing

This recipe is ideal for small amounts of royal icing required to create embroidery, brush embroidery, lace and other piped techniques.

Ingredients

1 medium free-range egg white, at room temperature
225 g (8 oz/1¾ cups) icing sugar, sifted

Wash the mixer bowl and the beater with a concentrated detergent and then scald with boiling water to remove any traces of grease and leftover detergent. Dry thoroughly.

Place the egg white into the mixer bowl with the majority of the icing sugar and mix the two together with a metal spoon.

Fix the bowl and beater to the machine and beat on the lowest speed until the icing has reached full peak - this takes about 8 minutes. You may need to add a little extra sugar if the mixture is too soft.

Cold porcelain

This is an inedible air-drying craft paste that can be used in almost exactly the same way as flowerpaste. The bonus with this paste is that the flowers made from it are much stronger and less prone to breakages. However, because it is inedible, anything made from this paste cannot come into direct contact with a cake's surface, so flowers made from cold porcelain need to be placed in a vase, container, candle-holder or Perspex plaque. I tend to treat flowers made with this paste pretty much as I would fresh or silk flowers. There are several commercial cold porcelain pastes available but you can make your own - the recipe below is the one that I prefer. I prefer to use measuring spoons and measuring cups to measure out the ingredients.

Ingredients

2½ Tbsp baby oil
115 ml (4 fl oz/½ cup) hi-tack non-toxic craft glue (Impex)
115 ml (4 fl oz/½ cup) white PVA wood glue (Liberon Super wood glue or Elmers)
125 g (4½ oz/1 cup) cornflour
Permanent white artist's gouache paint

Work in a well-ventilated area when making this paste. Wear a filter mask if you suffer from asthma. Measure the baby oil and the two glues together in a non-stick saucepan to form an emulsion. Stir the cornflour into the mixture. It will go lumpy at this stage but this is normal!

Place the pan over a medium heat and stir the paste with a heavy-duty plastic or wooden spoon. The paste will gradually come away from the base and sides of the pan to form a ball around the spoon. Scrape any uncooked paste from the spoon and add it to the mix. The cooking time will vary - usually around 10 minutes – between gas, electric and ceramic hobs, but the general rule is the lower the heat and the slower you mix the paste, the smoother the resulting paste will be. I'm impatient so I tend to turn up the heat a little to cook faster. Keep on stirring the paste to cook it evenly. You will need to split the paste and press the inner parts of the ball against the heat of the pan to cook it too – be careful not to overcook.

Turn the paste onto a non-stick board and knead it until smooth. The paste is quite hot at this stage. The kneading should help distribute some heat through the paste to cook any undercooked areas. If the paste is very sticky then you will need to put it back in the pan.

Wrap in plastic wrap and leave to cool – moisture will build up on the surface of the paste that, if left, will encourage mould growth, so it is important to re-knead the paste when cool and then re-wrap. Place in a plastic food bag and then in an airtight container, and store at room temperature. This paste has been known to work well two years after it was made if stored like this.

Prior to making flowers you will need to add a smidgen of permanent white gouache paint. The paste looks white but by its very nature dries clear, giving a translucence to the finished flower. Adding the paint makes the finish more opaque. Handling the paste is quite similar to working with sugar except I use cold cream cleanser instead of white vegetable fat, and glue or anti-bacterial wipes/water to moisten the petals to stick them. Cornflour is used as for handling flowerpaste. The paste shrinks a little as it dries – this is because of the glue. This can be disconcerting to begin with but you will gradually get used to it and it can be an advantage when making miniature flowers.

Flowerpaste

I always buy ready-made commercial flowerpaste (APOC) as it tends to be more consistent than homemade pastes. The following recipe is the one I used prior to discovering the joys of ready-made flowerpaste! Gum tragacanth gives the paste stretch and strength too. It can also be mixed with sugarpaste to produce a modelling paste suitable for small models and bas-relief designs.

Ingredients

5 tsp cold water
2 tsp powdered gelatine
500 g (1 lb 2 oz/3 cups) icing sugar, sifted
3 tsp gum tragacanth
2 tsp liquid glucose
3 tsp white vegetable fat, plus 1 extra tsp to add later
1 large fresh egg white

Mix the cold water and gelatine together in a small bowl and leave to stand for 30 minutes. Sift the icing sugar and gum tragacanth together into the bowl of a heavy-duty mixer and fit it to the machine.

Place the bowl with the gelatine mixture over a saucepan of hot water and stir until the gelatine has dissolved. Warm a teaspoon in hot water and then measure out the liquid glucose – the heat of the spoon should help to ease the glucose on its way. Add the glucose and 3 teaspoons of white fat to the gelatine mixture, and continue to heat until all the ingredients have dissolved and are thoroughly mixed together.

Add the dissolved gelatine mixture to the icing sugar/gum tragacanth with the egg white. Beat at the mixer's lowest speed, then gradually increase the speed to maximum until the paste is white and stringy.

Remove the paste from the bowl, knead into a smooth ball and cover with the remaining teaspoon of white fat – this helps to prevent the paste forming a dry crust that can leave hard bits in the paste at the rolling out stage. Place in a plastic food bag and store in an airtight container. Allow the paste to rest and mature for 12 hours before use.

The paste should be well-kneaded before you start to roll it out or model it into a flower shape, otherwise it has a tendency to dry out and crack around the edges. This is an air-drying paste so when you are not using it make sure it is well wrapped in a plastic bag. If you have cut out lots of petals, cover them over with a plastic bag.

Techniques

There are some essential techniques that you will use time and time again when creating cake and floral designs. Here are the ones that I use the most.

Coating a cake with almond paste

I adore the flavour and texture of almond paste. A layer of natural-coloured white almond paste gives a smooth, round-edged base on which to apply a layer of sugarpaste, creating a more professional finish and excellent eating quality too! It is important that the work surface is free of flour or cornflour, as if any gets trapped between the almond paste and the sugarpaste it can cause fermentation, encouraging air bubbles. It is best, but not always essential, to leave the almond paste-coated cake to dry out and firm up for a few days prior to icing.

1 Before applying any form of coating, the cake must be level. To do this, carefully cut off the top of the cake if it has formed a dome during baking. Then turn the cake upside down so that the flat bottom becomes the top. Fill any large indentations with almond paste if required. Place the cake onto a thin cake board the same size as the cake so that it is easier to move. You might also prefer to add a strip of almond paste around the base of the cake to seal it and the cake board tightly together.

2 Warm some apricot jam and a dash of water, brandy or Cointreau, and then sieve to make an apricot glaze that can be painted onto the surface of the cake. This will help to stick the almond paste to the cake and help seal it to keep it fresh. Apricot glaze is used as the colour is not too dark and the flavour tends not to fight with the taste of the cake or almond paste. You may also be able to buy ready-sieved apricot glaze in a jar – which also benefits from a dash of alcohol.

3 You will need a long, non-stick rolling pin large enough to roll out almond paste to cover at least a 30 cm (12 in) cake. Plastic smoothers are also essential to create a professional finish: a curved smoother for the top of the cake and a square-edged one for the sides. Rolling out almond paste to an even thickness can be tricky, and a novice cake decorator might find a pair of marzipan spacers useful to roll against. Depending which way they are placed, they can produce thick or thin sheets of almond paste/sugarpaste. It is best to store the paste in a warm place prior to kneading to help soften it slightly – otherwise it can be quite hard to work with. Knead the paste on a clean, dry surface to make it pliable.

4 Lightly dust the work surface with icing sugar. Place the almond paste on top and if needed position the spacers on either side of the paste. Roll the paste out lengthways using the non-stick rolling pin. Turn it sideways and reposition the spacers on either side again. Continue to roll out the paste until it is large enough to cover the cake. A measuring tape, string or even using the length of the rolling pin to gauge the exact size of the cake top and its sides can be useful. It is always best to allow slightly more than you think you will need, especially for awkward-shaped cakes or anything with corners to it.

5 Using a round-edged plastic smoother, polish and smooth out the surface of the almond paste. Start gently, gradually increasing the pressure to even out any slightly uneven areas of the paste.

6 Place the rolling pin on top of the almond paste and use it to help lift the paste over the cake. Remove the rolling pin and ease the almond paste into place. Smooth the surface of the cake to exclude any air bubbles. Tuck the paste to fit the sides. If you are working on a cake with corners, then concentrate on these first of all.

7 Use the curved-edge smoother to polish the top of the cake. Use strong, firm hand movements to 'iron out' any imperfections. Use the edge of the straight-edged smoother to cut and flick away the excess paste from the base of the cake. Finally, use the straight-edged smoother to iron out the sides of

the cake using a fair amount of pressure. Place the cake onto a sheet of greaseproof paper and, if time allows, leave to firm up overnight or for a few days prior to coating with sugarpaste.

Coating a cake and cake drum with sugarpaste

Plastic sugarpaste smoothers are essential when covering a cake with sugarpaste. The round-edged smoother is good for working on the top of the cake and the straight-edged smoother is good for working on the sides, giving a sharper edge at the base. Covering a cake with sugarpaste is a fairly straightforward process - however, practice is needed to achieve very neat results. If you are colouring the sugarpaste it is best to use paste food colour or to thicken liquid colours with icing sugar. It is safer to colour a small amount of sugarpaste and then knead this into the larger amount of paste to control the depth of colour rather than create a paste that is too brightly coloured.

1 Knead the sugarpaste on a clean, dry sugar- and flour-free surface until smooth and pliable. Take care not to knead in too many air bubbles. When fully kneaded, lightly dust the work surface with sieved icing sugar and place the sugarpaste on top, with any cracks against the work surface. Roll out, smooth and polish the paste as described for the almond paste coating.

2 Moisten the surface of the almond paste with clear alcohol (Cointreau, kirsch or white rum can all be used). Use a sponge to apply the alcohol as this gives a more even covering. Any dry areas will encourage air bubbles to be trapped between the almond paste and the sugarpaste. The alcohol helps to stick the sugarpaste to the almond paste and also acts as an antibacterial agent.

3 Pick up the sugarpaste onto the rolling pin and lower it over the cake, taking care to position the paste so that it will cover the sides evenly. Remove the rolling pin. Use your hands and then the round-edged smoother to create a smooth finish and eliminate air bubbles. Next, lift and ease the paste against the sides of the cake. If the cake has corners or points, deal with these first as they often crack or tear. Be careful not to stretch the sugarpaste too much as you work. Trim the excess paste from the base of the cake using a flat knife or the edge of a straight-edged smoother. Use the same smoother to iron out the sides of the cake. Use a pin to prick any air bubbles/pockets that might appear (brightly coloured glass head pins are best for this job so that you can easily spot them when not in use) and then smooth over with the sugarpaste smoothers. Continue to use the curved-edge smoother on the top of the cake and the straight-edged smoother on the sides to create a good, even finish. The edges of the coating or any difficult points or curved areas can be given extra attention with a pad of sugarpaste pressed into the palm of your hand and used to polish the paste.

4 To coat a cake drum, roll out the sugarpaste and carefully place it over a drum moistened with clear alcohol. Smooth over with the round-edged smoother and then trim off the excess with a flat knife. Smooth the cut edge with a smoother to neaten it. Next, polish with a pad of sugarpaste pressed into the palm of your hand.

5 Soften a small amount of sugarpaste with clear alcohol (Cointreau, kirsch or white rum) and place at the centre of the cake drum. Carefully lower the cake which should already be on a cake board of the same size over the top. Gently press down the top of the cake with the round-edged smoother to bond the cake and the drum together. Use the straight-edged smoother to blend and create a good join between the cake and the drum. Smooth over any areas that need extra attention with the sugarpaste pad technique.

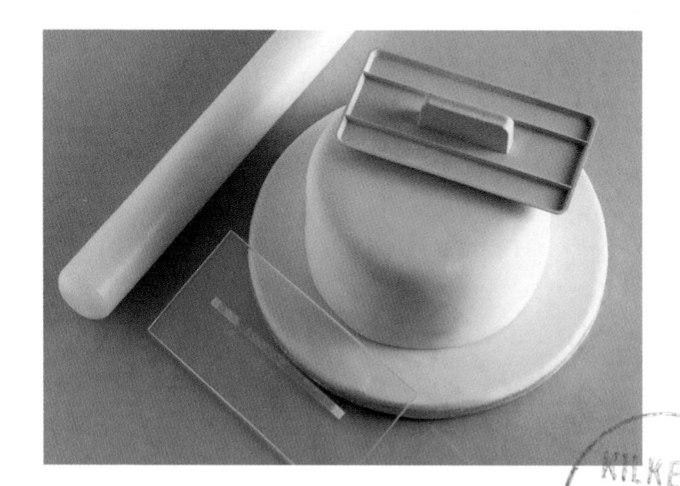

Wiring petals and leaves

This is my favourite method of constructing flowers. It gives the flowers much more movement and extra strength too, resulting in fewer breakages.

1 Knead a piece of flowerpaste and form roughly into the shape of the petal or leaf you are making. Press it down against a non-stick board to flatten it slightly. Use a celstick or rolling pin to roll the flowerpaste, leaving a ridge for the wire. Try to create a tapered ridge, angling the pin slightly so that the ridge is thicker at the base of the petal/leaf. The thickness and length of the ridge will depend on the size of the petal/leaf you are making. There are also boards available commercially which have grooves in them that create a similar ridged effect when the paste is rolled over them. These can be great for smaller petals and leaves but I find they produce too fine a ridge for many of the larger flowers that I make.

2 Cut out the petal/leaf shape using a cutter, scalpel or plain-edge cutting wheel, leaving the ridge to run down the centre. If you are using a cutter, lift up the shape and place it onto a very light dusting of cornflour and then press firmly with the cutter and scrub it slightly against the paste and the board so that the shape remains slightly stuck in the cutter. This will enable you to quickly rub the edge of the cutter to create a cleaner-cut edge, removing any fuzzy bits.

3 Moisten the wire very slightly with fresh egg white – too much will result in the paper coming off the wire and also slow down the drying process of the petal on the wire. Hold the ridge firmly between your finger and thumb, and hold the wire in the other hand very close to the end of the wire that is being inserted into the shape. Push the wire in gradually so that it supports a third to half the length. Use a ball tool to soften and thin the edge of the shape using a rolling action, working the tool half on your hand/foam pad and half on the edge of the paste.

4 Place the petal/leaf into a double-sided petal/leaf veiner and press the two sides firmly against the shape to texture it.

5 A frilled edge can be added using a cocktail stick or a ceramic veining tool, working at intervals to encourage a natural frilled effect.

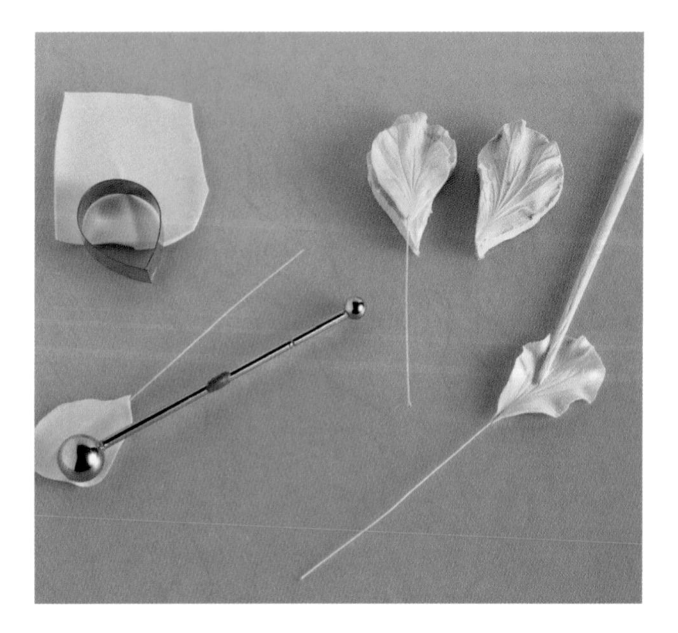

Glazing

Glazing can help give a leaf or petal a more realistic appearance. Care must be taken not to glaze flowers too heavily as this can make them look unnatural.

Steaming

Using powder colours on sugar flowers often leaves a slightly dry-looking finished flower; this can be changed to create a slightly more waxy appearance and also help to set the colour to stop it leaving marks on the surface of the coated cake. Hold each flower in the steam from a boiling kettle for a few seconds, or until the surface turns slightly shiny. Take care not to scald yourself and also not to get the sugar too wet as it will dissolve fairly fast. Allow the flower to dry before wiring into a spray. If you are trying to create a velvety finish to something like a red rose, then use the steaming process and then re-dust the flower – you will find that this will hold onto more dust, producing the desired effect.

Edible gold and silver leaf

Sheets of 23-carat gold and silver leaf to embellish side designs are perfect for Christmas/festive cakes. However, the sheets are very fine and tend to tear and fly very easily. Using the following method creates a more convenient way to control this delightful trickster!

1 Roll out some well-kneaded flowerpaste very thinly using a non-stick rolling pin. Lift up the paste and place the sticky side that was against the non-stick board carefully over a whole single sheet of gold/silver leaf. Smooth the flowerpaste from behind onto the leaf to adhere the two together. Turn the flowerpaste over to reveal the coated side. Trim off the excess uncoated paste from the edges. Leave to set for about 20 minutes to give a more paper-like finish and then cut out shapes using a paper punch or flower/leaf cutters. Keep any leftover pieces of the gilded paste to use at a later stage – these dried pieces of paste can be broken into small shards and used to create an alternative decorative effect combined with painted images, added to piped embroidery designs or even combined with dragées.

2 A crackle effect can also be achieved by resting the gold/silver leaf-coated flowerpaste a little and then re-rolling to reveal the colour of the flowerpaste beneath – this can be particularly effective using purple, red or black flowerpaste as a backing for gold or silver leaf.

3 For a jewelled, textured effect, sprinkle some coloured sugar crystal sprinkles on top of the freshly bonded gold/silver leaf flowerpaste and then quickly roll this into the surface using a non-stick rolling pin to embed the crystals into the paste.

FLOWERS AND FOLIAGE

The Christmas rose (*Helleborus niger*) is always a welcome delight during the winter months. There are many other forms of hellebore too, with spotted outer sepals and a large colour range from white through to cream, yellow, orange, red, purple and almost black, making it a very versatile addition to the flowermaker's repertoire. The plant has a romantic history – for centuries it was thought to cure madness and counteract witchcraft! In fact, still today, they are often planted outside doorsteps to ward off evil spirits.

Materials

- 35-, 33-, 30-, 28-, 26-, 24- and 22-gauge white wires
- Pale green cold porcelain
- Nile green floristry tape
- Vine, aubergine, plum, sunflower, daffodil, edelweiss, white, forest and foliage petal dusts
- Small white seed-head stamens
- Hi-tack non-toxic craft glue
- Pale green flowerpaste
- Fresh egg white
- White and mid-green flowerpaste
- Edible spray varnish (Fabilo)

Equipment

- Wire cutters
- Dusting brushes
- Scissors
- Tweezers
- Dresden tool (J)
- Smooth ceramic tool
- Non-stick board
- Non-stick rolling pin
- Large Christmas rose cutter (TT282)
- Foam pad
- Large metal ball tool
- Cupped Christmas rose veiner (SKGI)
- Fine-nose pliers
- Hellebore leaf veiner (ADV)
- Fine scissors
- Large briar rose leaf veiner (SKGI)
- Scalpel or plain-edge cutting wheel

Pistil

1 This section is made up from five sections joined together to form the fruiting body of the plant. Once the flower has been pollinated, these individual sections become much more inflated in shape. The flower described here is for a fairly newly opened flower. This can be represented using five short lengths of twisted nile green floristry tape, or as I prefer to do it, using cold porcelain-coated wires. Cut five lengths of 33-, or if you can obtain it, 35-gauge white wire. Blend a tiny ball of pale green cold porcelain onto the end of the wire and work it so that the base is broad and the tip at the end of the wire is very fine: it should measure between 1.5 and 2 cm (5/8 and 3/4 in) in length; this does vary a little between varieties. Smooth the cold porcelain between your finger and thumb and then against your palm to create a neat finish. Pinch a gentle ridge at the broader base area.

Repeat to make five sections. As the cold porcelain firms up it becomes easier to curve the tips back slightly. Tape the five sections together with quarter-width nile green floristry tape. Dust lightly with vine and tinge the tips with aubergine and plum petal dusts mixed together; again this colouring does vary a little between varieties.

Stamens

2 Divide half to three-quarters of a bunch of small white seed-head stamens into five or six smaller groups. Line up their tips and then bond each group at the centre using a small amount of hi-tack non-toxic craft glue. Squeeze the glue from the centre towards both ends, leaving an area at both ends unglued. Flatten each bunch as you work and try not to use too much glue as this creates bulk and takes too long to dry. It is also important that the glue forms a fairly straight line. Allow the glue to dry and then cut each group in half with scissors. Trim off some of the excess glue at the base so that when measured the stamens are fractionally shorter than the pistil.

3 Apply a tiny amount of hi-tack non-toxic craft glue to the base of each group of stamens and then position and squeeze each group to secure the stamens in place. Keep cleaning your fingers as any dried glue encourages the next group of stamens to stick to you and not the pistil! Holding each group and squeezing it against the pistil counting to ten helps to give enough time for the glue to grip well. Repeat with the other groups until you have achieved the desired effect. This is another area where some flowers have more stamens than others. Allow to dry and then curve the stamens out slightly around the edges using tweezers. Dust the tips of the stamens with a mixture of sunflower and daffodil petal dusts. Dust the base of the stamens with vine.

Nectaries (petals)

4 This is where things get a little confusing! The larger petal-like shapes are actually sepals (sort of modified bracts) and the true petals are actually formed into very small tubular nectaries that are held right at the base of the stamens. In a more mature flower, as the ovary inflates, both the stamens and nectaries drop off. Temptation is to leave them off but this does affect the final result. A quicker effect can be achieved using an eight-petal daisy shape or similar to cut out an all-in-one shape. However, over the years I just find that it looks so much better if each nectary is made individually. Form a tiny ball of well-kneaded pale green flowerpaste into a cone shape. Hollow out the broad end using the broad end of the Dresden tool or the smooth ceramic tool.

5 Work the flowerpaste against the non-stick board to encourage the lower part of the nectary to flatten more and create a lip. Repeat to make ten (eight if you are saving time!) nectaries. Attach to the base of the stamens using fresh egg white or an edible glue made from mashing flowerpaste and fresh egg white together. The other option is to make these nectaries using cold porcelain and attaching them with hi-tack craft glue. (Note: not for competition work though!) Allow to dry and then dust the nectaries with vine petal dust. Tinges of aubergine and plum petal dusts can add a little interest too.

Sepals

6 As mentioned above, these are not the true petals in the flower! Roll out some well-kneaded white flowerpaste, leaving a thick ridge for the wire. The sepals are not too fine so be careful not to roll the flowerpaste very fine. Cut out the sepal shape using the large Christmas rose cutter. There is a bump at the base of the cutter – this is the end where the wire will be inserted in.

7 Moisten the end of 28-gauge white wire with fresh egg white and gradually insert it into the thick ridge, supporting the ridge firmly between your finger and thumb. The wire should support about a third of the length of the sepal.

8 Place the sepal on your palm or onto a firm foam pad and soften the edges gently using the large metal ball tool – do not apply too much pressure as this will create a frilled effect which you don't want.

9 Place the sepal into the double-sided cupped Christmas rose veiner and press firmly to texture the surface. Remove from the veiner and pinch the sepal at the base and gently at the tip and also rub the centre to create a gentle cupped shape. Repeat to make five sepals.

Assembly and colouring

10 It is best to assemble the flower while the paste is still slightly pliable. Tape two of the sepals onto the base of the stamens and nectaries using quarter-width nile green floristry tape so that they have a slight gap between them. Next, add a petal behind these two to fill the gap. Add the remaining two to fill the larger gap at the base of the flower. Take care not to create a spiralled effect! Add a 22-gauge white wire to the stem and tape over with half-width nile green floristry tape.

11 Tinge the base of each sepal inside and out with a light mixture of edelweiss and vine petal dusts. Some flowers have more green on them as they age. Tinge the edges if desired with a mixture of plum and edelweiss petal dusts. This colouring is generally where the sunlight hits the flower on the back of its sepals.

12 Hold the back of the flower with fine-nose pliers and then bend the flower head downwards slightly. Add a few small leaves at the top of the stem (see steps 15–17). Dust the stem with aubergine and plum petal dusts mixed together. Spray the stem lightly with edible spray varnish to seal the colour. Once the flower has dried, steam it to create a slightly waxy finish.

Buds

13 Tape over a half-length of 22-gauge white wire with half-width nile green floristry tape and then bend a hook in the end using fine-nose pliers. Moisten the hook with fresh egg white and insert it into the base of a cone-shaped piece of well-kneaded white flowerpaste. Work the base of the cone into a slight point between your finger and thumb.

14 Pinch three outer sepals from the side of the bud using your finger and thumb. Thin the edges if needed and then twist the sepals around to create a neat bud shape. Dust with a mixture of vine and white. Add a tinge of plum and edelweiss to the upper side of the bud. Hold the wire directly behind the bud with fine-nose pliers and bend as for the flower. Add two or three small leaves at the bend.

Small leaves

15 There are a few small leaves directly behind each flower and bud. These can be made quickly using the 'twiddle and splat' method. Blend a ball of mid-green flowerpaste onto the end of a 30- or 28-gauge white wire. Form a fine point at the tip and at the base. These leaves vary in length on each flower and also between different varieties. Smooth between your palms and then place the wired shape onto the non-stick board. Splat/flatten the shape using the flat side of the hellebore leaf veiner. Remove the veiner and carefully remove the leaf from the board. If the edges are untidy, simply trim them with fine scissors. With time and practice you will find it easier to create a smoothness to the shape prior to splatting that creates a neater final result.

16 Soften the edge of the leaf to thin it a little more and then place in the double-sided large briar rose leaf veiner to texture it. Remove from the veiner and then pinch the leaf from the base to the tip to accentuate the central vein.

17 Use fine scissors to cut a series of fine serrations to the edges of the leaf. Give the leaf a gentle curve at the tip. Repeat to make numerous small leaves.

Larger leaves

18 These are grouped in sets of five, rather like a hand shape: one large, two slightly smaller and two smaller again. Roll out some mid-green flowerpaste not too thinly, leaving a thick ridge for the wire. Cut out a freehand leaf shape using the scalpel or plain-edge cutting wheel or there is a template on p 106 to refer to if you prefer.

19 Insert a 26- or 24-gauge white wire, depending on the size of the leaf you are making. Support the thick ridge as you insert it and try to support about half the length of the leaf. Soften the edge using the metal ball tool and then place it into the double-sided hellebore leaf veiner and press firmly to texture. Remove from the veiner and pinch the leaf from the base to the tip to accentuate the central vein, curving the leaf a little to give some movement too. Repeat to make leaves in sets of five. Allow to dry fairly flat with a slight curve at the tips.

Colouring

20 It is best to dust the leaves before they have dried so that the colour sticks faster and is more intense than if you dust when they are very dry. Dust in layers, gently at first with forest fading towards the edges and then heavier with foliage petal dust. The backs of the leaves are dusted a lighter green using what is left on the brush. Tinge the edges with aubergine mixed with plum petal dust. Allow to dry.

21 Tape the leaves together, starting with the large leaf, followed by two smaller ones on either side and then two smaller leaves at the base using half-width nile green floristry tape. Dust the main stem on the upper surface with a mixture of plum and aubergine. Spray lightly with edible spray varnish.

Silver tillandsia

Otherwise known as air plant, *Tillandsia xerographica* from South America is a great leaf to add shape and an unusual structure to a bouquet or arrangement. The soft silvery leaves are an ideal colour to add to Christmas displays.

Materials

- Pale green flowerpaste
- 26- and 24-gauge white wires
- Fresh egg white
- Edelweiss, foliage, forest and aubergine petal dusts
- White bridal satin dust
- White floristry tape

Equipment

- Non-stick rolling pin
- Scalpel or plain-edge cutting wheel
- Foam pad
- Large ball tool
- Stargazer B petal veiner
- Non-stick board
- Dusting brushes

1 Roll out some pale green flowerpaste, leaving a thick ridge for the wire. Cut out the long, slender pointed leaf shape using a freehand technique with a scalpel or plain-edge cutting wheel.

2 Insert a 26- or 24-gauge white wire moistened with fresh egg white into the thick ridge to support about half to three-quarters of the length of the leaf. Place the leaf onto a firm foam pad and use the large ball tool to soften the edges.

3 Next, place the leaf into the double-sided stargazer B petal veiner and press firmly to texture. Remove the leaf from the veiner and pinch from the base through to the tip, curving and curling the stem into shape to give interesting movement. Repeat to make leaves in varying sizes.

4 An alternative method is to work a ball of pale green flowerpaste onto a white wire, blending it into a finer point towards the end of the wire. Flatten the shape against the non-stick board using the flat side of the stargazer B petal veiner. Soften the edges, vein, pinch and shape as above. This method gives more variation in size and shape.

Colouring

5 Mix together edelweiss petal dust with a touch of foliage and forest to make a very light greyish green. Use this mixture to colour each leaf from the base to the tip on both sides. Tinge the base and tip edges with aubergine petal dust. Over-dust each leaf with white bridal satin dust.

6 Tape into groups using half-width white floristry tape or use the foliage individually. Hold over a jet of steam from a kettle or clothes steamer to set the colour and take away the very dry finish left by the layers of petal dust.

Materials

- 33-, 30-, 28-, 26-, 22-gauge white wires
- Pale green and white flowerpaste
- Fresh egg white
- Nile green and brown floristry tape
- Vine, white, plum, foliage, aubergine and white bridal satin petal dusts
- Edible spray varnish (Fabilo)

Equipment

- Tea light
- Fine-nose pliers
- Dusting brushes
- Non-stick rolling pin
- Simple leaf cutters (TT)
- Plain-edge cutting wheel (PME)
- Snowberry leaf veiner (SKGI)

Snowberries

This deciduous shrub was introduced to Britain in the 19th century. There are about 15 species of *Symphoricarpus* that originate from Northern and Central America, and one species that is from China. The globular snowball-like fruit is mostly white, or white tinged with green or pink.

Berries

1 Burn the tape from the end of several short 33-gauge white wires. The berries are small, green and slightly oval in shape. Form some well-kneaded pale green flowerpaste into tiny oval shapes and insert a 33-gauge white wire moistened with fresh egg white into each shape so that the wire protrudes very slightly. This is to represent what is left of the calyx. For the larger white berries, burn more wires – 30- or 28-gauge, depending on the size you are making. For added bulk to the calyx, bend a tiny hook in the end of each short length of wire using fine-nose pliers prior to burning the tape off. Roll balls of well-kneaded white flowerpaste in graduating sizes. Moisten the burnt end of the wire with fresh egg white and insert into the berry so that once again the tip protrudes very slightly. Leave to dry.

2 Tape the small green ovaries together using quarter-width nile green floristry tape, gradually adding a 26-gauge white wire if more strength is needed, and introduce the smaller white berries graduating to the larger ones. Dust the ovaries with a light mixture of vine and white petal dusts. Add tinges to the white berries too. If you are tinging with pink, then mix together plum and white, and gently catch the berries with colour. Over-dust with white bridal satin.

3 Tape the leaves in pairs down the stem, starting with the smallest and graduating in size as you work. If you are creating larger stems, add these small groups onto a 22-gauge white wire using half-width brown floristry tape. Spray the berries with edible spray varnish or steam to set the colour.

Leaves

4 Roll out some pale green flowerpaste, leaving a thick ridge for the wire. Cut out the leaf using a simple leaf cutter or plain-edge cutting wheel. Insert a 30-, 28- or 26-gauge white wire into the pointed end of the leaf to support about half the length of the leaf.

5 Soften the edge of the leaf and vein using the snowberry leaf veiner. Remove from the veiner and pinch from the base to the tip to accentuate the central vein. Repeat to make leaves in pairs of graduating sizes.

6 Dust the upper surface with vine and foliage petal dusts; the smaller leaves should be brighter in colour. Some varieties have tinges of aubergine. Keep the back of the leaves paler.

Larch cones

The larch tree drops its needles as winter approaches, allowing the cones to become more prominent. There are Japanese and European larch trees as well as this hybrid version. Larches were first brought from central Europe to Britain in 1620 as a ornamental trees.

Materials

- 26- and 24-gauge white wires
- Light brown flowerpaste
- Fresh egg white
- Brown, nutkin, black and foliage petal dusts
- Edible spray varnish
- Nile green and brown floristry tape

Equipment

- Fine-nose pliers
- Non-stick rolling pin
- Brodea cutters (TT)
- Ceramic silk veining tool or blunt cocktail stick
- Small ball tool
- Dusting brushes

1 Bend a hook in the end of a 26-gauge white wire using fine-nose pliers. Attach a ball of light brown flowerpaste to the end of the hook, which should be moistened with fresh egg white. Leave to dry overnight if time allows.

2 Roll out some light brown flowerpaste fairly thinly and cut out several shapes using the brodea cutters – the number of cut-out shapes required will depend on how large you are making the cones. I tend to make some small, medium and large cones to form a twig. Use the ceramic silk veining tool or a blunt cocktail stick to work on each of the six sections to broaden and thin them out.

3 Hollow out the centre of each section using the small ball tool. Moisten the centre with fresh egg white and thread the first layer up onto the back of the wired dried cone. Snuggle each of the sections around the dried cone, trying not to spiral them.

4 Continue to work on each layer in the same way, threading it onto the back of the previous layer to cover joins. Pinch behind each shape to create a space or add an extra tiny ball of flowerpaste as you work to give more breathing space to each layer. Gradually increase the size of the layers as you work. Allow to dry a little before dusting with colour.

5 Dust the cones with a mixture of brown, nutkin and black petal dusts. Spray lightly with edible spray varnish or steam to set the colour.

6 If you decide to add needles to the twigs for autumnal or early winter displays, these can be created by twisting quarter-width nile green floristry tape back onto itself. Repeat to make numerous needles and squeeze together into small groups.

7 To create a twig, tape over a 24-gauge white wire with half-width brown floristry tape. Add extra layers to thicken the twig. Next, twist and squeeze short lengths of half-width brown floristry tape back onto itself to form small bud-like formations. Tape these alternating down the twig. Add needles if desired and then gradually introduce the cones graduating in size. Dust the needles with foliage and the twig with nutkin and black petal dusts. Add extra wires as you work down the stem to thicken it if needed.

Winter jasmine

Jasminium nudiflorum is originally from China but it is more than a welcome delight in many European gardens, being one of the few winter plants to produce such brightly coloured flowers in what is generally a fairly bleak period, weather-wise.

Materials

- Pale yellow and pale green flowerpaste
- 28-, 26- and 22-gauge white wires
- Fresh egg white
- Fine white stamens
- Daffodil, sunflower and vine petal dusts
- Nile green floristry tape

Equipment

- Non-stick board
- Smooth ceramic tool
- Brodea cutters (TT917, 918)
- Small ball tool
- Fine-nose pliers
- Dusting brushes
- Tweezers
- Tiny six-petal pointed blossom cutter (OP)

Flower

1 Form a cone-shaped piece of pale yellow flowerpaste and then pinch the broad end to form a hat shape. Place the brim of the shape against the non-stick board and use the smooth ceramic tool to roll and thin it out. Cut out the flower shape using either of the brodea cutters. It is best if you slightly scrub the cutter against the paste and the board so that the paste sticks in the cutter. Then pick it up and rub your thumb over the edge of the cutter to create a cleaner cut. Carefully release the petals from the cutter.

2 Place the shape back against the non-stick board and broaden and elongate each petal slightly, using a rolling action with the broader end of the smooth ceramic tool. Use the pointed end of the tool to open up the throat.

3 Hollow out the back of each petal slightly, using the small ball tool. Next, using fine-nose pliers, bend a hook in the end of a 26-gauge white wire. Moisten the hook with fresh egg white and thread the wire through the centre of the flower. Work the flowerpaste between your finger and thumb to create a more slender shaped neck and pinch off any excess at the base. Tweak the petals a little to give the flower shape some movement. Insert a short white stamen into the centre of the flower to represent the pistil. Allow to dry a little before colouring. Dust the flower with a mixture of daffodil and a touch of sunflower petal dusts. Add a tinge of vine petal dust to the pistil and centre of the flower.

Bud

4 Form a cone-shaped piece of pale yellow flowerpaste and insert a 28- or 26-gauge white wire into the base of the cone. Thin down the broad base between your finger and thumb to create an elongated neck to the bud. Pinch a few petals around the tip of the bud, using tweezers or your finger and thumb, and then twist them around back on themselves to create the impression of spiralled petals. Repeat to make buds in varying sizes. Dust to match the flower. Roll out some pale green flowerpaste thinly and cut out several calyces using the tiny six-petal pointed blossom cutter. Soften the edges and attach a calyx onto the back of each flower and bud. Use half-width nile green floristry tape to tape the buds and the flowers onto 22-gauge white wire to form twiggy stems.

Holly

Holly leaves are quite difficult to replicate in sugar due to the extreme sharp points and also lack of natural veining in the real leaf. The holly pictured here is a smaller variety that fits in well with most Christmas floral displays.

Materials

- 33-, 30-, 28-, 26- and 24-gauge white wires
- Red and mid-green flowerpaste
- Fresh egg white
- Ruby, red, aubergine, woodland, forest, foliage and vine petal dusts
- Edible spray varnish
- Nile green floristry tape

Equipment

- Wire cutters
- Fine-nose pliers
- Tea light
- Dusting brushes
- Non-stick rolling pin
- Holly leaf cutters (AP) or (OP)
- Holly 'hedgehog' leaf veiner (SKGI)

Berries

1 Cut short lengths of 33-gauge white wire. Bend a hook in the end of each wire using fine-nose pliers. Burn the hooked end of the wires with the flame of a tea light to blacken it. This will form the centre of each holly berry.

2 Roll several small balls of red flowerpaste to make the berries. Moisten a hooked wire with fresh egg white at the singed end and thread through the centre of a berry. Repeat to make the required number of berries. Allow to firm up a little before colouring.

3 Dust the berries with ruby and red petal dusts. Tinges of aubergine can also be added to give a little variation. Spray with edible spray varnish. You might need a few coats of glaze to give a good sheen.

Leaves

4 Roll out some mid-green flowerpaste, leaving a thick ridge for the wire. Holly leaves are quite fleshy so try not to roll the paste too fine. Cut out the leaf shapes using the holly leaf cutters.

5 Insert a 30-, 28-, 26- or 24-gauge white wire moistened with fresh egg white into the thick ridge to support about half the length of the leaf. Soften the edge of the leaf and then vein using the holly leaf veiner.

6 Pinch and twist each of the points in the edge of the leaf to give a spiky appearance. Repeat to make the required number of leaves in varying sizes.

7 Dust the leaves heavily on the upper surface with woodland, forest and foliage petal dusts. Tinge the edges with a little aubergine petal dust. Dust the back of the leaf with foliage and vine petal dusts. Leave to dry and then spray with edible spray varnish to give a glossy finish. Tape the berries into small groups using half-width nile green floristry tape. Tape over each of the leaf wires with the same tape and then add the leaves around the berries as required.

Ivy

Along with holly, ivy is one of the most iconic Christmas symbols. For the flowermaker, it is a very versatile foliage for adding to many celebration designs.

Materials

- Pale green flowerpaste
- 30-, 28-, 26-, 24- and 22-gauge white wires
- Fresh egg white
- Foliage, forest, woodland, aubergine, moss and black petal dusts
- Edible spray varnish or half-glaze
- Nile green and beige or brown floristry tape

Equipment

- Non-stick rolling pin
- Pointed ivy cutters (J)
- Birdsfoot ivy leaf veiners (SKGI)
- Dusting brushes
- Scalpel or scriber
- Wire cutters
- Fine angled tweezers

Leaves

1 There are many different varieties of ivy. The one described here is a fine pointed form called birdsfoot. Roll out some pale green flowerpaste, leaving a thick ridge for the wire. Cut out the leaf using one of the four sizes of pointed ivy cutters.

2 Insert a 28- or 26-gauge white wire moistened with fresh egg white into the thick ridge to support about half the length of the leaf; the gauge of the wire will depend on the size of leaf you are making. Soften the edge of the leaf and then texture it using the double-sided ivy leaf veiner. Remove from the veiner and pinch from the base to the tip to accentuate the central vein. Pinch each of the side sections too and give the tips a slight curve here and there if you wish. Repeat to make the required number of leaves.

3 Dust the leaves with foliage petal dust and over-dust with forest and woodland to add a little depth. Tinge the edges with aubergine. Allow the leaves to dry overnight before glazing with edible spray varnish or dipping into a half-glaze.

4 Once the glaze has dried, you have the option of creating fine paler veins on each leaf. This is done by etching through the glaze and into the surface of the flowerpaste with a scalpel or scriber to reveal the pale green flowerpaste. Take care not to apply too much pressure as this will break the leaf. Scribe the main veins first and then add finer side veins.

Assembly

5 Tape over about 2.5 cm (1 in) of each leaf stem with quarter-width nile green floristry tape. Tape over the end of a 24-gauge white wire with half-width beige or brown floristry tape. Curve and curl the tip slightly and then start adding the small leaves to the main stem, leaving a little of each leaf stem showing. Work from one side to the other, adding the leaves graduating in size as you work down the stem. Add an extra 24- or 22-gauge white wire as you work down longer stems to add length and support.

Ivy berries

6 Cut short lengths of 30-gauge white wire. Roll small balls of pale green flowerpaste and insert a wire moistened with fresh egg white so that it almost comes out the other end, forming a sharp point. Add an extra pinch if the point is not sharp enough. Use fine angled tweezers to pinch a pentagon shape around the top of the berry. Repeat to make numerous berries.

7 Tape over each stem with quarter-width nile green floristry tape and then tape the stems into clusters. Dust with moss petal dust on the sides and a mixture of black and aubergine on the top.

Hippeastrum

This unusual hippeastrum flower is very useful for adding another green dimension to bouquets and arrangements. Hippeastrums are native to South America and were originally incorrectly grouped by botanists with the amaryllis family which are native to South Africa!

Materials

- 28-, 26- and 24-gauge white wires
- Pale vine green and white flowerpaste
- Vine, sunflower, moss, plum and aubergine petal dusts
- Fresh egg white
- Nile green floristry tape
- Isopropyl alcohol

Equipment

- Fine curved scissors
- Dusting brushes, including large flat brush
- Wire cutters
- Plain-edge cutting wheel (PME)
- Non-stick rolling pin
- Wide amaryllis petal veiner (SKGI)
- Fine paintbrush

Pistil

1 Insert a length of 26-gauge white wire into a ball of pale vine green flowerpaste and work it quickly down the wire to create the required length – it should be slightly shorter than the shortest hippeastrum petal template on p 106. Smooth the pistil between your palms and then pinch off any excess. Try to work a little of the flowerpaste so that it stands beyond the tip of the wire and then cut into three sections using fine curved scissors. Pinch each section to neaten and then curl the tips back. Bend the length into a very lazy 'S' shape. Dust with vine petal dust, leaving the split ends very pale.

Stamens

2 Cut two lengths of 28-gauge white wire into thirds to create six stamens. Attach a small ball of pale vine green flowerpaste 5 cm (2½ in) from the tip of the wire and then blend and work it to the tip to create a fine filament. Pinch off any excess flowerpaste. Smooth the length between your palms to create a neater finish. Repeat to make six stamens. Curve each stamen to follow the line of the pistil.

3 For the anther, form a small sausage shape of white flowerpaste and attach it to the end of the stamen using a small amount of fresh egg white. The size of the anther depends on how mature the flower is (mature flowers have smaller anthers). Use the scalpel or plain-edge cutting wheel to draw a line down the central length of the anther. Repeat with the other stamens. Dust the anther with sunflower petal dust and the length of each filament with vine green.

4 Tape the six stamens on to the pistil using half-width nile green floristry tape. If the filaments/stamens are still pliable, you will be able to reshape them to follow the exact line of the pistil.

Petals

5 The inner petals and outer sepals of the flower are all made in the same way, varying the size to make three large outer sepals, two slightly smaller petals and one smaller again. Roll out some well-kneaded pale vine green flowerpaste, leaving a thick ridge for the wire. Place the hippeastrum petal template on p 106 on top of the

flowerpaste with the thick ridge running down the centre and cut around it using the scalpel or plain-edge cutting wheel.

6 Insert a 24-gauge white wire moistened with fresh egg white into the thick ridge to support about half the length of the petal/sepal. Soften the edge of the shape and then place into the double-sided wide amaryllis petal veiner to texture. Remove from the veiner and pinch from the base through to the tip to accentuate the central vein and also give the petal a curve. Repeat with the other petal/sepal shapes and allow them to firm up a little before dusting and assembling the flower.

Colouring and assembly

7 Dust each petal and sepal with vine and tinges of vine mixed with moss petal dusts. Tape the two larger petals onto the stamens/pistil using half-width nile green floristry tape. Add the smaller petal underneath the stamens. Next, tape in the three large sepals so that they sit in between the petals and are slightly recessed. If the flowerpaste is still pliable, you will be able to reshape the flower to create a more realistic effect.

8 Add detail markings to the petals using a mixture of plum and aubergine petal dusts and a fine paintbrush. Tinge the edges of the petals and sepals using the same mixture and a larger flat brush. Next, dilute some aubergine with isopropyl alcohol to paint a series of finer lines onto the larger petals. Allow to dry and then hold over a jet of steam to set the colour and give the petals a slight shine.

Red amaryllis

Although this flower belongs to the hippeastrum family, it is still commonly and affectionately known as the amaryllis. Anyway, the method is almost the same for both. The flower pictured here is one of the smaller varieties with wide petals. The colour variation is vast – I prefer red flowers for Christmas and always seem to have them as a cut flower in my home over the festive period.

Materials

- Pale poppy-coloured flowerpaste
- Ruby, sunflower and aubergine petal dusts
- Nile green floristry tape
- 28-, 26-, 24- and 20-gauge white wires

Equipment

- Dusting brushes
- Amaryllis petal cutters (TT) or hippeastrum templates on p 106
- Non-stick rolling pin
- Scalpel or plain-edge cutting wheel
- Large metal ball tool
- Wide amaryllis petal veiner (SKGI)

Stamens and pistil

1 These are made in exactly the same way as the stamens described for the hippeastrum on pages 30–31 (see steps 2 to 4), except the flowerpaste is a pale poppy colour. Dust the pistil with ruby petal dust, leaving the very tip much paler. Dust the length of each stamen with ruby and then dust the anthers with sunflower petal dust. Tape the stamens and pistil together using half-width nile green floristry tape.

Inner petals

2 There are two sizes of petal cutter in the amaryllis set. You will need to make two large petals and one small petal. Roll out some poppy-coloured flowerpaste not too thinly and cut out a large petal shape using the large amaryllis petal cutter or the hippeastrum template on p 106 and a scalpel or plain-edge cutting wheel. Insert a 26-gauge white wire into the thick ridge to support about half the length of the petal.

3 Soften the edge of the petal using the large metal ball tool and then vein using the wide amaryllis petal veiner. Remove from the veiner and pinch from the base to the tip to give a central vein and a slight curve too. Repeat the process to make another large petal, which should be a mirror image of the first one, and then continue to make a third smaller petal using the smaller cutter in the set.

Outer sepals

4 Repeat the above process but this time use 24-gauge white wires and the larger cutter in the amaryllis petal cutter set to create three large wide sepals.

5 Dust as desired. Here I have used ruby petal dust to give a strong colour, adding tinges of aubergine to the very edges. It is best to dust the petals/sepals while they are still pliable to achieve stronger colouring. Next, tape the two large petals onto either side of the stamens using half-width nile green floristry tape. Tape the smaller petal below the stamens. Complete the outer layer, taping the three large sepals to fit in between the positions of the inner three petals using half-width nile green floristry tape. While they are still pliable, re-shape the petals/sepals to create a more relaxed flower. Tape onto a 20-gauge white wire using half-width nile green floristry tape to add length and strength to the flower.

Japanese clerodendron berries

These very unusual blue berries are the fruit of *Clerodendron trichotomum* that follow a very pretty white flower with a pink calyx. The plant often loses its foliage when the berries are fully ripened.

Materials

28-gauge white wires
Green and plum flowerpaste
Fresh egg white
Hydrangea, gentian, black and plum petal dusts
Edible spray varnish
Nile green floristry tape

Equipment

Fine-nose pliers
Plain-edge cutting wheel or scalpel
Dusting brushes
Non-stick rolling pin
Small calyx cutter (TT)
Celstick or ceramic tool
Small ball tool
Dresden tool (J)

Berry

1 Bend a hook in the end of a short length of 28-gauge white wire using fine-nose pliers. Roll a small ball of well-kneaded green flowerpaste. Moisten the hooked end with fresh egg white and insert it into the ball. Pinch it around the wire to make sure it is secured well. Use the plain-edge cutting wheel or scalpel to divide the berry into four sections – these occur in even and uneven sections on one plant. Allow to firm up a little before dusting.

2 The berries ripen from green through to a bright dense blue so it depends what stage you are trying to recreate as to how much colour you use. Mix hydrangea and gentian petal dusts together with a touch of black, and colour the berry as desired. Allow to dry before spraying with edible spray varnish. Repeat to create the required number of berries. Leave to dry.

Calyx

3 Roll out some plum flowerpaste, leaving a raised pimple at the centre. Cut out the calyx shape using the small calyx cutter. Rub your thumb over the flowerpaste against the cutter to create a clean-cut edge.

4 Elongate and broaden each sepal using the celstick or ceramic tool. Hollow out the back of each sepal using the small ball tool.

5 Mark several indents using the plain-edge cutting wheel or Dresden tool onto the upper surface of the shape. Moisten the centre with fresh egg white and thread onto the back of the berry. Pinch the thicker pimple against the wire to secure the two together. Curve the sepals back and curl the tips if desired. Allow to firm up before dusting with plum petal dust.

6 Tape over each stem with quarter-width nile green floristry tape and then tape them together into clusters. Dust the stems with plum petal dust.

Materials

- Poppy-coloured and white flowerpaste
- 30-, 28-, 26- and 22-gauge white wires
- Fresh egg white
- White and nile green floristry tape
- Coral, ruby, sunflower, white, aubergine, edelweiss, forest and vine petal dusts
- Isopropyl alcohol

Equipment

- Smooth ceramic tool
- Small ball tool
- Fine angled tweezers
- Non-stick board
- Stargazer B petal veiner
- Fine sharp scissors
- Plain-edge cutting wheel
- Dusting brushes
- Fine paintbrush
- Fine-nose pliers

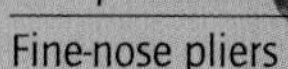

Flame orchid

There are 15 species of renanthera orchid, sometimes known as flame or fire orchids, found throughout Malaysia, Indonesia, the Philippines and New Guinea. I have used freehand techniques to make this orchid, as although there are cutters available, I find this method gives a more interesting end result. The size of the orchid varies between varieties and there also tends to be a slight size variation on one stem too.

Column

1 Roll a small ball of poppy-coloured flowerpaste and form it into a cone shape. Insert a 28-gauge white wire moistened with fresh egg white into the fine end of the cone. Hollow out the underside of the column by pressing it against the rounded end of the smooth ceramic tool, pinching a gentle ridge at the back of the column. Leave to dry overnight. If time allows, attach a small ball of white flowerpaste to the tip of the underside of the column and split into two sections to represent the anther cap.

Lip/labellum

2 Form a teardrop-shaped piece of poppy-coloured flowerpaste and then pinch out the broad end to form two 'ears'. Pinch and thin the ears, and pinch and flatten the pointed lip section. Next, hollow out the ears using the small ball tool.

3 Use fine angled tweezers to pinch two ridges onto the lip. Pinch a protrusion on the underside of the base of the shape between the two ears.

4 Moisten the base of the column with fresh egg white and attach the lip so that the ears wrap around the side of the column, making sure there is still a space between the underside of the column and the top of the lip. Curve the pointed end of the lip and set aside while you work on the outer petals.

Lateral petals (wing petals)

5 Insert a 30-gauge white wire moistened with fresh egg white into a small ball of poppy-coloured flowerpaste and work the paste down the wire to create a fine petal shape, forming the tip of the shape into a slight point. Place the shape on the non-stick board and flatten using the flat side of the stargazer B petal veiner. Trim off any excess using fine sharp scissors and then soften the edge with the small ball tool.

6 Texture the surface of the petal using the double-sided stargazer B petal veiner. Repeat to make a second petal. While they are still pliable, pinch the base of each petal backwards slightly to give a curled edge.

Dorsal sepal (head)

7 The dorsal sepal is made in the same way as the lateral petals but it is slightly longer and broader in shape. Once again, pinch the base of the sepal back at the base and curve the tip forwards slightly.

Lateral sepals (legs)

8 These are much longer and broader than any of the other sections. Use 28-gauge white wire to form the lateral sepals in the same way as the lateral petals but use more poppy-coloured flowerpaste to obtain the broader shape required. Curve each shape so that it forms a bow-legged appearance.

Assembly

9 It is best to assemble the orchid while the petals/sepals are still pliable so that you can reshape the flower to create a more relaxed finish. Position and tape the two small lateral petals onto either side of the column and labellum using quarter-width white floristry tape. Add the slightly longer dorsal sepal in between the lateral petals and finally add the lateral sepals at the base of the orchid.

10 Attach a ball of poppy-coloured flowerpaste behind the flower and work it down the stem to create a fleshier stem between the flower and the main stem. Texture the length using the plain-edge cutting wheel.

Colouring

11 Dust each of the outer petals and sepals heavily on the front with a mixture of coral and ruby petal dusts. Some varieties have yellow lateral petals and others have tinges of yellow at the base of each petal/sepal. The variety I have chosen to make here only had a touch of sunflower on the underside of the labellum. The back of each petal/sepal should be kept much paler and dusted with a light mixture of sunflower and white petal dusts. Dust the edges and the pointed lip of the labellum with ruby petal dust.

12 Next, dilute some ruby petal dust with isopropyl alcohol to add some depth onto the lip and also some spots onto the lateral sepals using a fine paintbrush. Tinge the edges of the petals with a dry mixture of aubergine and ruby petal dusts.

Buds

13 Using fine-nose pliers, bend a hook in the end of a 28- or 26-gauge white wire, depending on the size of bud you are making. Form a ball of poppy-coloured flowerpaste and insert the hooked wire moistened with fresh egg white into the base. Pinch it onto the wire to create a strong join. Pinch a small node/protrusion at the base of the bud. Use the plain-edge cutting wheel to mark the lines to give the impression of petals tightly clasped together. Repeat to make buds in graduating sizes.

14 Dust lightly with coral and ruby petal dusts and then add tinges of edelweiss/sunflower and an over-dusting of forest/vine, especially to the smallest buds.

15 Tape the buds using half-width nile green floristry tape, starting with the smallest onto a 22-gauge white wire. Alternate the buds as you add them down the stem, leaving quite a bit of each individual stem showing. Gradually add the flowers, graduating their size a little too. Steam the whole stem to set the colour and give a slight sheen.

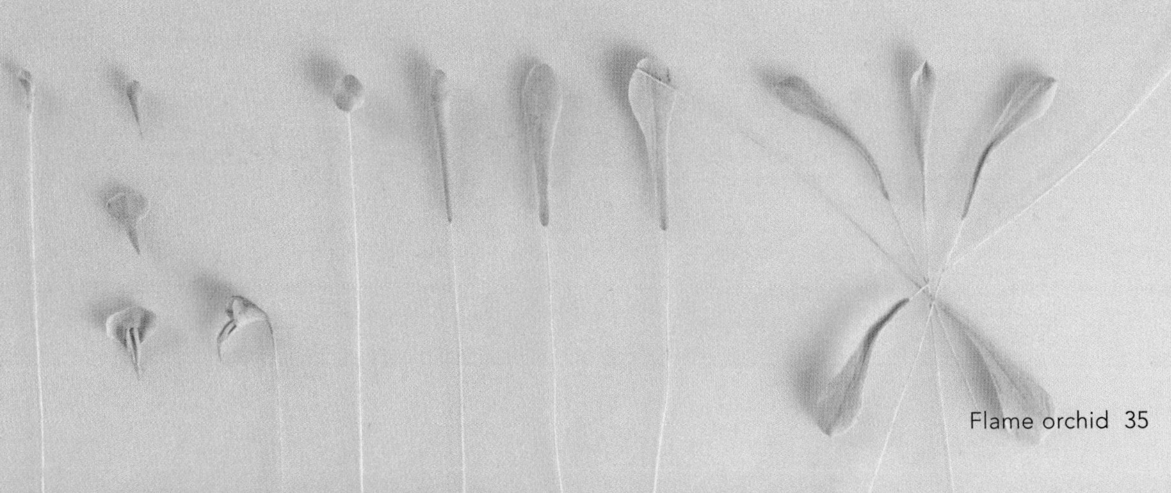

Dried lotus pods

These are the dried seed receptacles from the East Indian lotus flower (*Nelumbo nuciflora*). They make a useful addition to festive displays and provide an interesting texture and rustic charm. They can also look wonderful coloured gold or silver for Christmas displays.

Materials

- 18-, 20- and 22-gauge white wires
- Pale cream flowerpaste
- Black, brown, nutkin and aubergine petal dusts
- Fresh egg white
- Brown floristry tape
- Edible spray varnish (Fabilo)

Equipment

- Fine-nose pliers
- Large celstick
- Tea light
- Angled tweezers
- Plain-edge cutting wheel
- Fine scissors
- Flat dusting brushes
- Non-stick rolling pin
- Smooth ceramic tool

1 Using fine-nose pliers, bend a large hook in the end of a strong white wire – the gauge of the wire will depend on the size of pod you are making. Roll a ball of well-kneaded pale cream flowerpaste and form it into a cone shape.

2 Use the large celstick to open up the broad end of the cone. Keep pressing the paste against the celstick to thin out the shape and turn it into almost a large acorn cup shape.

3 Next, heat the hooked end of the wire with the flame of a tea light until red hot. Quickly thread the cold end of the wire through the centre of the cup shape and then pull the hot end into the thick area at the centre of the cup – the idea is that the hot wire caramelizes the sugar and cools quickly, creating a quick and strong bond. You can always use fresh egg white instead but this takes longer to dry. While the paste is still pliable, create a series of grooves and ridges on the side of the cup using angled tweezers and the plain-edge cutting wheel. Using fine scissors, trim off any irregular excess from the top edge of the cup so that it is fairly level.

4 Dust the inside of the cup with black petal dust. You might want to include some dried balls of flowerpaste in the cup so that once the lid is placed on top it rattles. Roll out some more flowerpaste not too thinly. Moisten the edge of the cup with fresh egg white and turn it down on top of the rolled-out paste. Carefully trim around the paste using the plain-edge cutting wheel. Pinch the two edges together to make sure the lid is securely in place. Pinch around the rim with angled tweezers.

5 Use the pointed end of the smooth ceramic tool to create a series of irregular placed/sized holes. Tape over the main stem with half-width brown floristry tape.

6 Dust with brown, nutkin and tinges of black and aubergine petal dusts. Allow to dry and then steam or spray very lightly with edible spray varnish.

Ilex berries

Ilex verticillata is a native holly from America and Canada. The plant loses its foliage during the autumn, allowing these glossy berries to shine brightly on naked stems. The berries can be yellow, orange or as described here red, making them a very useful addition to festive displays for cakes.

Materials

- 35-, 33-, 22-, 20- and 18-gauge white wires
- Red flowerpaste
- Fresh egg white
- Red, ruby, foliage, aubergine and nutkin petal dusts
- Edible spray varnish
- Brown floristry tape

Equipment

- Wire cutters
- Fine-nose pliers
- Tea light
- Flat dusting brushes

Berries

1 Cut 35- or 33-gauge white wire into five or six short lengths. Take five or six short wires at a time and line up the ends to then bend them all in one fail swoop using fine-nose pliers.

2 Burn the hooked end of the wires with the flame of a tea light to blacken them.

3 Roll balls of red flowerpaste to make the berries. Moisten the hook with fresh egg white and pull through a single wire into each ball. Leave to firm up a little before the next stage.

4 Dust the berries to create the desired effect. Here, I have dusted in layers with red and ruby petal dusts. Allow to dry and then spray with edible spray varnish or dip into a full glaze. You might need a few layers of glaze to create very shiny berries. Allow to dry. Dust the short stems with foliage and aubergine petal dusts.

5 Tape over a short length of 22-gauge white wire with half-width brown floristry tape to create a twig effect. Tape the berries tightly onto the twig. To create a larger piece, tape several smaller twigs onto a 20- or 18-gauge white wire.

6 Dust the twigs carefully with nutkin petal dust. Be very careful not to catch the berries too much with this colour. Spray lightly again with edible spray varnish.

Silver philodendron

These silver-spotted trailing leaves are wonderful for adding detail and filling large spaces in an arrangement or bouquet. The silver spots on the leaves add an instant festive frosted feel. Here, I have made some of the smaller foliage on the plant but the leaves can be quite large at about 10 cm (4 in) in length.

Materials

- Mid-green flowerpaste
- 26-, 24-, 22- and 20-gauge white wires
- Fresh egg white
- Foliage, forest, edelweiss, myrtle bridal satin and aubergine petal dusts
- Isopropyl alcohol
- Nile green floristry tape
- Edible spray varnish (Fabilo)

Equipment

- Non-stick rolling pin
- Heart-shaped leaf cutters, or templates on p 107
- Scalpel or plain-edge cutting wheel
- Foam pad
- Large metal ball tool
- Dimpled foam or crumpled kitchen paper
- Dusting brushes

1 Roll out some mid-green flowerpaste not too thinly, leaving a thicker area at the centre for the wire. Cut out the leaf shape using one of the heart-shaped leaf cutters or the templates on p 107 and a scalpel or plain-edge cutting wheel.

2 Insert a 26-, 24- or 22-gauge white wire moistened with fresh egg white into the thick ridge to support about half the length of the leaf. Place the leaf onto a firm foam pad or your palm and soften the edge using a rolling action with the large metal ball tool.

3 Pinch the leaf from the base to the tip to create a central vein and give the leaf more movement at. Allow to dry over some dimpled foam or crumpled kitchen paper to help give the leaf a little support and shape. Repeat to make leaves in graduating sizes.

Colouring and assembly

4 Dust the leaves with a mixture of foliage, forest and edelweiss petal dusts. Dilute some myrtle bridal satin petal dust with isopropyl alcohol and paint a series of irregular-sized dots. Add tinges of aubergine to the edges of each leaf.

5 Tape over each stem with half-width nile green floristry tape. Start taping a trailing stem together, starting with a small leaf on the end of a 22- or 20-gauge white using half-width nile green floristry tape at first, adding the other leaves so that they alternate down the stem, gradually working with full-width floristry tape to create fleshier stems as the leaves increase in size. Bend the length of the main stem to create an attractive bend and curve. Spray lightly with edible spray varnish.

Maranta

There are over 20 species of maranta from tropical America. The common name of 'Prayer plant' is given to the plant because of the way the younger foliage folds up in the evening. The red veins make it one of my favourite types of foliage to use in Christmas arrangements and bouquets.

Materials

- Pale green flowerpaste
- 24- and 22-gauge white wires
- Fresh egg white
- Nile green floristry tape
- Ruby, vine, foliage, forest, plum and aubergine petal dusts
- Isopropyl alcohol
- Edible spray varnish (Fabilo)

Equipment

- Non-stick rolling pin
- Scalpel or plain-edge cutting wheel
- Foam pad
- Large ball tool
- Maranta or calathea leaf veiner (SKGI)
- Fine paintbrushes
- Flat dusting brushes

1 Roll out some well-kneaded pale green flowerpaste, leaving a thick ridge at the centre for the wire. Cut out the leaf shape either freehand or using the templates on p 107 and a scalpel or plain-edge cutting wheel.

2 Insert a 24- or 22-gauge white wire moistened with fresh egg white into the thick ridge of the leaf to support about half the length of the leaf. Place the leaf onto a firm foam pad and soften the edge using a rolling action with the large ball tool.

3 Place the leaf into the double-sided maranta or calathea leaf veiner. Press the veiner firmly to create a strong texture on the surface of the leaf.

4 Remove the leaf from the veiner and pinch it from behind at the base to the tip to accentuate the central vein. Allow to firm up a little before colouring. Tape over the main stem with half-width nile green floristry tape. Add extra 22-gauge white wire if you want to add strength to, or elongate, the stem.

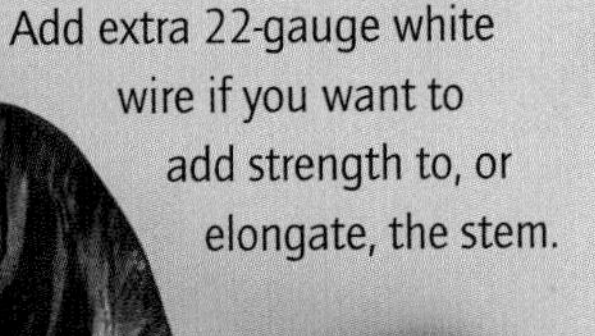

Colouring

5 Mix together ruby petal dust with isopropyl alcohol and paint a central vein down the front of the leaf using a fine paintbrush. Add finer side veins using the same mixture. Allow to dry. Next, dust a line of vine petal dust down the centre of the leaf on either side of the main red central vein, taking care not to cover over the red veins too much.

6 Use a flat dusting brush to work some foliage petal dust from the edges of the leaf towards the centre, working in between each of the margins created by the red veins. Leave a paler area at the base of each margin where the vine green colouring is. Next, dilute some foliage and forest petal dusts with isopropyl alcohol and paint heavy green markings in between the finer red veins. Add this colour to the edge to create a border. Leave to dry.

7 Dust the back of the leaf with a mixture of plum and aubergine petal dusts. Over-dust areas of the upper surface with foliage petal dust to calm down the painted design a little. Add a tinge of aubergine and plum petal dusts here and there to the edges of the upper surface. Spray very lightly with edible spray varnish.

Poinsettia

The poinsettia (*Euphorbia pulcherrima*) is one of the most popular plants used to decorate the home at Christmastime and sugar versions look stunning on cakes. Although poinsettias have become readily accepted as an almost traditional Christmas flower, they actually have exotic roots as they originate from Mexico! The eye-catching part of the plant is not its tiny flowers but the large, ornate bracts which surround them: these are actually colourful modified leaves. In the wild, the plant is usually a creamy white, red or slight variations in between. Hybridized forms are now available in coral, cream and pink, and there is even a bluish form that has recently become available too. Care must be taken when handling the plant as the stems secrete a white poisonous sap when snapped.

Materials

- 120-gauge fine white cotton thread (Apoc)
- 35-, 33-, 30-, 28-, 26-, 24- and 20-gauge white wires
- Nile green floristry tape
- Vine, moss, ruby, sunflower, daffodil, red, foliage, forest, woodland, edelweiss and aubergine petal dusts
- Fresh egg white
- Mimosa sugartex or semolina coloured with yellow petal dust
- Pale green, yellow, red and mid-green flowerpaste
- Isopropyl alcohol

Equipment

- Wire cutters
- Fine-nose pliers
- Fine scissors
- Emery board
- Dusting brushes, including flat dusting brushes
- Non-stick board
- Scalpel
- Non-stick rolling pin
- Poinsettia cutter set (J) or templates on p 108
- Plain-edge cutting wheel
- Firm foam pad
- Large metal ball tool
- Poinsettia bract and leaf veiners (SKGI)
- Fine paintbrush

Stamens and flower centre

The real flowers of the poinsettia look rather like a series of complicated stamens at the heart of each group of coloured bracts. They are quite complicated in form so I tend to simplify them somewhat so that I can rush on to make the more attractive and eye-catching bracts. The number of buds and fully open flowers can vary at the centre of the bracts so if time is short, then use fewer flowers and more buds.

1 Wrap fine white 120-gauge white cotton thread about six or seven times around two slightly parted fingers to create a loop. Cut a third of a length of 33-gauge white wire (or 35-gauge wire if you can find it). Bend the wire

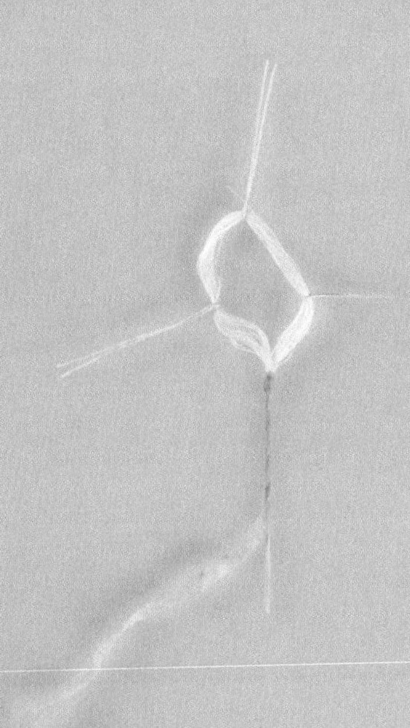

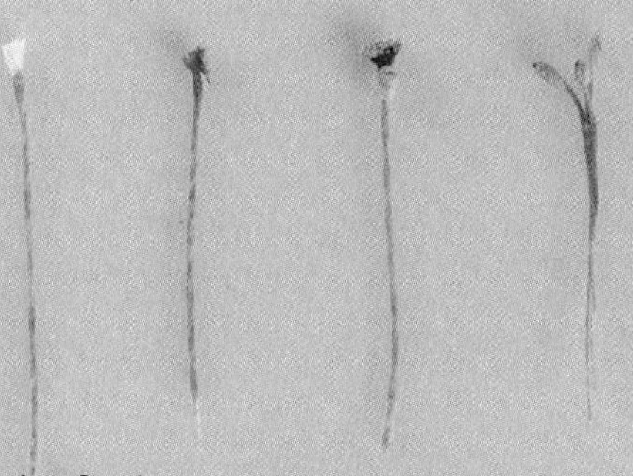

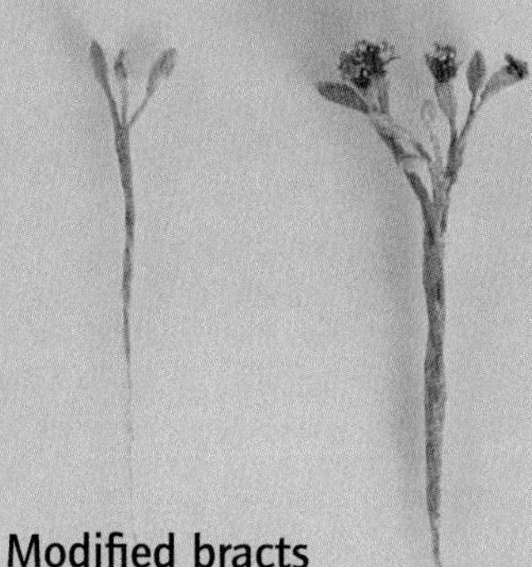

using fine-nose pliers to create a hairpin shape through the loop of thread and squeeze it tightly to hold the thread in place. Tape over the base of the thread and down onto the wires using quarter-width nile green floristry tape. Repeat this method around the loop with another three or four wires – the number of wires will depend on how big the loop is. Use fine scissors to cut through the thread to give short stamens to each wire. Trim them shorter if needed.

2 Rub the tips of thread against an emery board to fuzz them up slightly. Dust the threads as required: in a cream poinsettia, the thread should be coloured with vine and moss petal dusts; in a red form, the stamens are dusted with ruby petal dust.

3 Paint a layer of fresh egg white onto the non-stick board and then carefully dab the tips of the stamens into the egg white to moisten the tips. This will act as a glue when you dip the tips into either mimosa sugartex/pollen (this is a fine but granular coloured sugar available from most cake decorating shops), or you can use semolina coloured with yellow petal dust. Repeat to make several centres, then allow to dry.

4 Next, attach a ball of well-kneaded pale green flowerpaste around the base of the stamens. Leave to dry a little before dusting with vine and moss petal dusts. A tiny ball of yellow flowerpaste may be added at the base of the red stamens on top of the green section to represent the petals of the flower. The petals are small but fleshy and divided in half with a scalpel resulting in something that looks like lips. Dust with sunflower and daffodil petal dusts.

5 To create the buds, cut short lengths of 33- or 35-gauge white wire and bend a hook in the end of each with fine-nose pliers. Attach a tiny ball of pale green flowerpaste to the dry hook and work the ball against the wire to secure it well. Try to create a very slight point at both the tip and the base. Dust with vine and moss petal dusts.

6 Tape over each of the wires with quarter-width nile green tape. Next, tape various combinations of flowers and buds into sets of three or four and then tape these groups together to create a fairly open centre.

Modified bracts

7 Roll out some well-kneaded red flowerpaste, leaving a thick ridge down the centre for the wire. Try not to roll the paste too thinly as the poinsettia veiners have very strong veins that may cut through finer paste. Use one of the several sizes of poinsettia cutters to cut out a bract shape or cut out the shape using one of the bract/leaf templates on p 108 and a scalpel or plain-edge cutting wheel.

8 Hold the thick ridge of the bract between your finger and thumb to support it and then insert a white wire moistened with fresh egg white into the ridge to support about a third to half the length of the bract. The gauge of the wire will depend on the size of bract you are making: use a 33-gauge wire for the tiny bracts and gradually increase the gauge up to a 26-gauge for the larger bracts. Remember, the higher the gauge number the finer the wire! The thickness of the flowerpaste at the base of the bract is very useful to help create the stem at the base. Pinch the paste at the base and work it between your finger and thumb to create a paste-coated section over the wire. The length will vary from the tiny bracts through to the larger shapes.

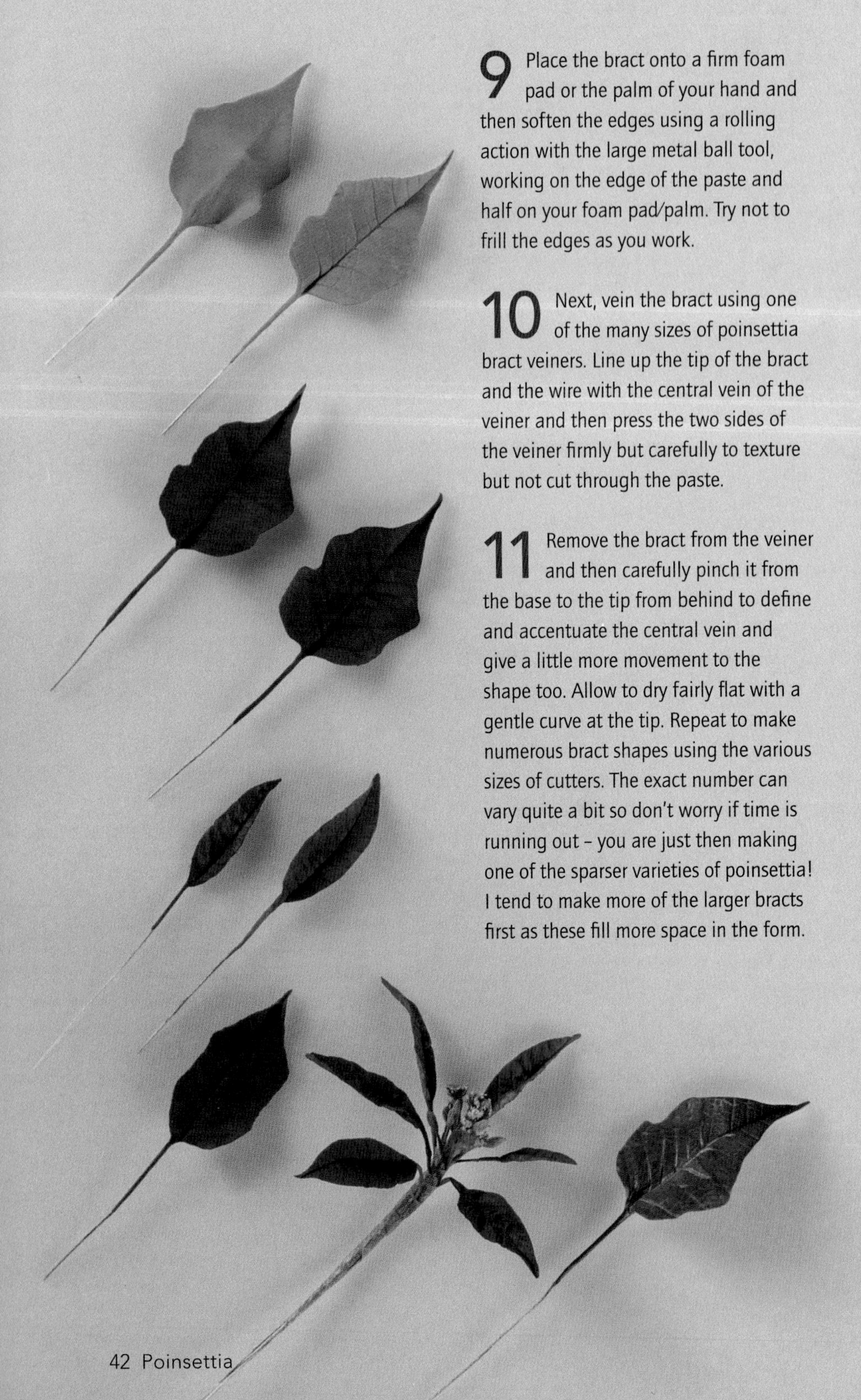

9 Place the bract onto a firm foam pad or the palm of your hand and then soften the edges using a rolling action with the large metal ball tool, working on the edge of the paste and half on your foam pad/palm. Try not to frill the edges as you work.

10 Next, vein the bract using one of the many sizes of poinsettia bract veiners. Line up the tip of the bract and the wire with the central vein of the veiner and then press the two sides of the veiner firmly but carefully to texture but not cut through the paste.

11 Remove the bract from the veiner and then carefully pinch it from the base to the tip from behind to define and accentuate the central vein and give a little more movement to the shape too. Allow to dry fairly flat with a gentle curve at the tip. Repeat to make numerous bract shapes using the various sizes of cutters. The exact number can vary quite a bit so don't worry if time is running out – you are just then making one of the sparser varieties of poinsettia! I tend to make more of the larger bracts first as these fill more space in the form.

Colouring

12 The exact colouring will depend on your taste: some of the red poinsettias are a very bright clean red, while others are duller with a heavy presence of green to them. Other forms are a very deep rich red. I prefer to dust the bracts for a red form with red and ruby petal dusts. Use a flat dusting brush to add colour from the base to the tip of the bract. Lightly dust the underside too. Repeat to colour all of the red bracts.

13 I prefer to add painted green veins to most of the bracts, regardless of their colour – it just helps to break up the solid colour a little and add more interest too. Use isopropyl alcohol to dilute some foliage petal dust and paint the fine veins onto each bract using a fine paintbrush. Taper the colour towards the edges of the bract. I tinge the bracts with a mixture of forest and foliage petal dusts too but I prefer to do this after it has been assembled as it is easier to balance the colour.

Assembly

14 Use quarter-width nile green floristry tape to start assembling the smallest bracts around the flower centre. Try to keep the formation fairly open, allowing each bract to drop slightly down the main stem as you add them. This is important to help create the fact that these are not petals forming a flower – if you get them too tight, the result looks more flower-like and reminds me of mass-produced silk flower forms! Increase the width of floristry tape to half-width as you add the larger bracts.

Leaves

15 Roll out some mid-green flowerpaste, leaving a thick ridge for the wire. Cut out the leaf shape using the largest of the poinsettia cutters from the set.

16 Insert a moistened 26- or 24-gauge white wire into the ridge to support about half the length of the leaf. Work the flowerpaste at the base of the leaf between your finger and thumb down onto the wire to create a slender thickened stem. Soften the edge using the large metal ball tool.

17 Vein using one of the larger poinsettia leaf veiners. Take care not to press too hard as the leaf veiners are even more defined than the bract veiners and do tend to cut through the paste if it is too fine. Pinch the leaf from the base to the tip to accentuate the central vein. Allow to dry as for the bracts – fairly flat with a slight curve at the tip.

18 Dust in layers, starting gently with forest and then woodland and finally foliage green. The back of the leaves are much paler. Dust the thickened stem at the base of the leaf with ruby petal dust. Add fine painted veins using a diluted mixture of isopropyl alcohol and edelweiss petal dust.

19 Tape the leaves around the red bracts, gradually working down the main stem. You might want to add a 20-gauge white wire at this stage if you are planning to use it in a large arrangement as this will give it more support.

20 Use foliage petal dust to tinge some of the red bracts on the back and the front. Use a mixture of ruby and aubergine to tinge the edges here and there on the green leaves. Steam the poinsettia to set the colour and take away the dry appearance left by the petal dusts.

Scarlet plume

Scarlet plume (*Euphorbia fulgens*), also known as shining euphorbia, is related to the poinsettia and shares the same trait of its petals looking like stamens and its bracts forming what look like its outer petals! Originally from Mexico, this plant is used quite a bit by florists and although the wild plant produces orange flowers, there are now hybridized forms with white, cream, yellow, salmon, deep orange and red apparent flowers.

Materials

- 120-gauge fine white cotton thread (Apoc)
- 33-, 28-, 26-, 22-gauge white wires
- Nile green floristry tape
- Vine, moss, ruby, red, foliage, forest, aubergine and edelweiss petal dusts
- Fresh egg white
- Mimosa sugartex or semolina coloured with yellow petal dust
- Poppy-coloured or pale lemon and mid-green flowerpaste
- Isopropyl alcohol
- Edible spray varnish (Fabilo)

Equipment

- Wire cutters
- Fine-nose pliers
- Fine scissors
- Emery board
- Dusting brushes
- Non-stick board
- Smooth ceramic tool or celstick
- Small five-petalled blossom cutter
- Small ball tool
- Scalpel
- Non-stick rolling pin
- Poinsettia cutter set (J)
- Poinsettia leaf veiner (SKGI)
- Fine paintbrush

Stamen-like flowers

1 Wrap fine white 120-gauge white cotton thread six or seven times around two slightly parted fingers to create a loop. Cut a third of a length of 33-gauge wire. Bend the wire using fine-nose pliers to create a hairpin shape through the loop of thread and squeeze it tightly to hold the thread in place. Tape over the base of the thread and down onto the wires using quarter-width nile green floristry tape. Repeat this method around the loop with another three or four wires – the number of wires will depend on how big the loop is. Use fine scissors to cut through the thread to give short stamens to each wire. Trim them shorter if needed.

2 Rub the tips of thread against an emery board to fuzz them up slightly. Dust the threads as required: in a cream flower form, the thread should be coloured with vine and moss petal dusts; in a red form, the stamens are dusted with ruby petal dust.

3 Paint a layer of fresh egg white onto the non-stick board and then carefully dab the tips of the stamens into the egg white to moisten the tips. This will act as a glue when you dip the tips into either mimosa sugartex/pollen (this is a fine but granular coloured sugar available from most cake decorating shops), or you can use semolina coloured with yellow petal dust. Repeat to make several centres, then allow to dry.

Flower-like bracts

4 The colour of the flowerpaste used for this section will depend on the colour variety you are making. Here, I am using pale poppy-coloured flowerpaste, but for cream, yellow, coral or orange varieties I prefer to use pale lemon flowerpaste and then dust to the required depth of colour. Form a ball of well-kneaded flowerpaste into a teardrop shape. Pinch the broad end of the teardrop between your finger and thumb to form a hat shape. Place the brim of the hat against the board and roll out around the thicker area using the smooth ceramic tool or a celstick.

5 Place the small five-petalled blossom cutter over the thick part of the hat and cut out the shape. Rub your thumb over the paste against the cutter before removing the shape to create a cleaner cut edge.

6 Carefully remove the shape from the cutter and then use the pointed end of the smooth ceramic tool to open up the centre. Place the blossom against the non-stick board and broaden each section slightly, using a rolling action with the smooth ceramic tool.

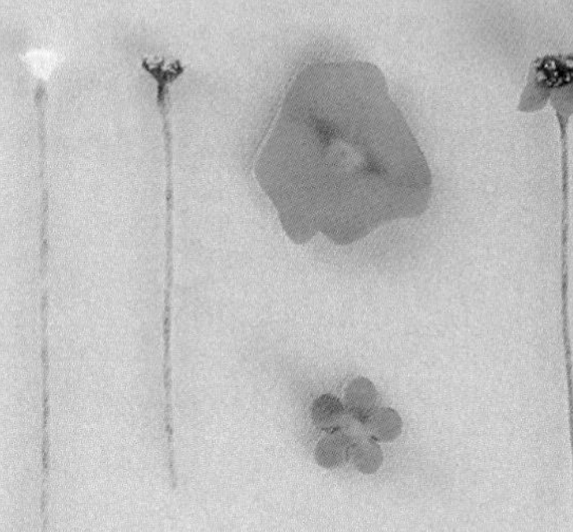

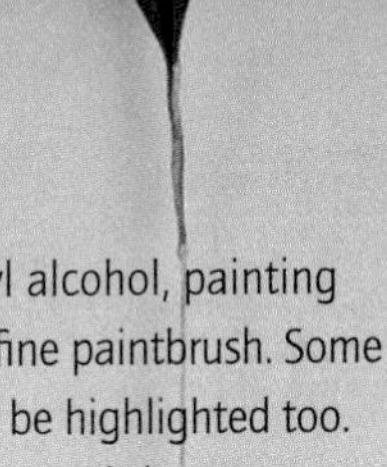

7 Next, hollow out the back of each of the five sections using the small ball tool or the rounded end of the smooth ceramic tool. Moisten the base of the thread centre with fresh egg white and thread it through the centre of the blossom/bract shape. Thin down the back a little between your finger and thumb and pinch off any excess. Repeat to make about 20 flowers per stem.

Buds

8 Cut several short lengths of 33-gauge white wire and then bend a hook in the end of each using fine-nose pliers. Insert the hook into the fine end of a small cone-shaped piece of flowerpaste. Thin the neck slightly and then divide the upper surface into five sections using the scalpel. Repeat to make numerous buds. Tape over each wire with quarter-width nile green floristry tape. Tape the buds and flowers into mixed groups of three.

Leaves

9 Roll out some mid-green flowerpaste, leaving a thick ridge for the wire. Cut out the leaf shape using one of the narrower leaf shapes from the poinsettia cutter set or use one of the templates on p 108 and cut around it using the scalpel or plain-edge cutting wheel. Insert a 28- or 26-gauge white wire into the thick ridge to support about half the length of the leaf – the gauge will depend on the size of leaf you are making.

10 Soften the edge of the leaf and then texture the leaf using the double-sided poinsettia leaf veiner, taking care not to press too firmly. Pinch the leaf from the base to the tip to accentuate the central vein and give movement. Repeat to make numerous leaves. Allow to firm a little before dusting with colour. Tape over each leaf stem with quarter-width nile green floristry tape.

Colouring and assembly

11 Dust the flower-like bracts with red and ruby petal dusts, keeping the backs a much paler version of the front. Dust the base of the flower with a mixture of foliage and vine petal dusts. Dust the buds to match the flowers.

12 Dust the leaves in layers with forest and then over-dust with foliage. The backs should be dusted very lightly. The edges are sometimes tinged with ruby/aubergine, depending on the variety. If time allows, highlight the central vein with a mixture of edelweiss, foliage and isopropyl alcohol, painting very carefully with a fine paintbrush. Some of the side veins may be highlighted too. Allow the leaves to dry and then spray lightly with edible spray varnish.

13 Tape a small leaf onto the end of a 22-gauge white wire using half-width nile green floristry tape, leaving part of its own stem showing. Introduce a group of buds accompanied by another leaf and continue working down the stem, adding groups of buds and flowers, and gradually increasing the size of the foliage as you add it to each group. Dust the stem with foliage. Steam to set the colour on the bracts.

Materials

- 30-, 28-, 26-, and 18-gauge white wires
- Nile green floristry tape
- White and holly/ivy flowerpaste
- Fresh egg white
- Vine, edelweiss, daffodil, sunflower, moss, foliage, forest, aubergine, plum and ruby petal dusts
- Edible spray varnish or half glaze (p 10)

Rose

I have always tried to incorporate roses into my books as they are still the most requested flower for cake decorators to make. This book is no exception. Roses make wonderful additions to Christmas displays, whether used as a focal flower or as a secondary flower with more seasonal flowers and foliage.

Equipment

- Fine-nose pliers
- Non-stick rolling pin
- Rose petal cutter set (TT549, 550, 551)
- Foam pad
- Metal ball tool (CC)
- Very large rose petal veiner (SKGI)
- Cornflour bag (p 9)
- Plastic food bag
- Smooth ceramic tool or cocktail stick
- Kitchen paper ring former (p 8)
- Dusting brushes
- Non-stick board
- Curved scissors
- Grooved board
- Rose leaf cutter (J)
- Large briar rose leaf veiner (SKGI)
- Set of three black rose leaf cutters (J)

Rose cone centre

1 Tape over a half to three-quarter length of 18-gauge white wire with half-width nile green floristry tape. Bend a large open hook in the end using fine-nose pliers. Form a ball of well-kneaded white flowerpaste into a cone shape to measure about two-thirds the length of the smallest rose petal cutter you are planning to use. Moisten the hook with fresh egg white and insert into the rounded base of the cone. Push the hook into most of the length of the cone. Pinch the base of the flowerpaste onto the wire to secure the two together. Reshape the point of the cone if required – I tend to form a sharp point with a more rounded base. Allow to dry for as long as possible.

2 Colour a large amount of white flowerpaste to the required colour; here I have used vine green petal dust to give a soft off-white base colour. I usually colour the paste paler than I want the finished rose to be.

First and second layers

3 Roll out some of the coloured flowerpaste fairly thinly using the non-stick rolling pin. Cut out four petals using the smaller of the two rose petal cutters you are planning to use. Place the petals on the foam pad and soften the edges using the metal ball tool – work half on the edge of the petal and half on the pad using a rolling action with the tool. Try not to frill the edges; at this stage you are only taking away the raw cut edge of the petal. Vein each of the petals in turn using the double-sided very large rose petal veiner – dust with a little cornflour if needed to prevent sticking, especially if the veiner is being used for the first time. For smaller roses it is not always essential to vein the petals but the larger flowers benefit from it greatly.

4 Place the first petal against the dried cone using a little fresh egg white to help stick it in place. It needs to be positioned quite high against the cone so that you have enough of the petal to curl tightly to form a spiral effect around the cone. It is important that this cone is not visible from the overview of the finished rose. Do not worry about covering the cone near the base – there are plenty more petals to follow that will do that job. I tend to curl the petal in from the left-hand side. Leave the right-hand edge of the petal slightly open so that the next petal can be tucked underneath it.

5 Moisten the remaining three petals with fresh egg white and start the second layer by tucking a petal underneath the first petal on the cone. Stick down the edge of the first petal over the new petal. Place the next petal over the join created and then turn the rose to add the third petal. I tend to keep these petals open to start with so that I can get the positioning correct before tightening them around the cone to form a spiral shape. Leave one of the petals open slightly to take the first petal of the next layer. Some roses have slightly pinched petals – this can be done as you add each layer by pinching the top edge to create a slight point. This number of petals can be used to make small rosebuds but the cone base should be made slightly smaller so that the petals cover the whole of it.

Third, fourth and fifth layers

6 Roll out some more coloured flowerpaste and cut out nine petals using the same size cutter as before. Soften the edges and vein the petals as before. Cover the petals with a plastic food bag to stop them drying out. Tuck the first petal underneath the open petal from the previous layer of the rosebud and continue to add the other petals as described above, attaching them in layers of three petals at a time. It is important to keep positioning petals over joins in the previous layer and not to line up petals directly behind each other. Gradually start to loosen the petals slightly as you work on the fourth and fifth layers. Pinch and curl the edges slightly more as you attach the fifth layer.

Sixth layer

7 Roll out some more coloured flowerpaste and cut out three petals using the slightly larger rose petal cutter. Soften and vein as before. This time, start to hollow out the centre of each petal using a large ball tool or by simply rubbing the petal with your thumb.

8 Moisten the base of each petal with fresh egg white, creating a 'V' shape. Attach to the rose as before, trying to place each petal over a join in the previous layer. Pinch either side of the petal at the base as you attach them so that it retains the cupped shape and allows the rose to breathe. Curl back the edges using the smooth ceramic tool, a cocktail stick or your fingers to create movement in the petal edges. I curl either edge of the petal to create a more pointed shape. You now have a 'half rose'.

Final layer

9 I prefer to wire the petals individually for the final layer of the rose; this gives more movement and a much stronger finished flower. Roll out some coloured flowerpaste, leaving a subtle ridge down the centre. Cut out the petal using the same size cutter as for the previous layer. Hook and moisten the end of a 26-gauge white wire. Insert it into the very base of the ridge. Soften the edges and vein as described previously. You will need cornflour dusting onto either the petal or the veiner to prevent the flowerpaste sticking to the veiner. Press the veiner firmly to create stronger veins. Remove from the veiner and hollow out the centre using your thumb and also start to curl back the edges. Allow the petal to dry slightly in a kitchen paper ring former. Repeat to make about eight to ten petals. As the petals are beginning to firm up, you can keep going back to add extra curls to the edges if required.

Assembly and colouring

10 I prefer to tape the individually wired petals around the half rose and then dust the rose as a whole – I balance the colour better this way. You might prefer to dust and then tape. It is best if the petals are not quite dry at this stage so that you can reshape them. Tape the first wired petal over a join in the petals of the half rose using half-width nile green floristry tape. The next petal is placed onto the opposite side of the rose and then continue adding the petals to cover gaps and joins in the previous layer. Try not to place petals in line with petals of the layer underneath.

11 Mix together edelweiss, vine, daffodil and sunflower petal dusts. Probe the flower with a brush loaded with this mix to add a 'glow' at the base of each petal on the back and front. I tend to be heavier with this colour on the back of the petals. The rose pictured has been dusted heavily with plum, with tinges of aubergine added to the very centre and edges of each petal. The back of each petal is slightly paler than the inside.

Calyx

12 As the outer petals of the rose have been individually wired it is best to wire each sepal of the calyx too. This gives a stronger finish but also allows the flowermaker to represent a calyx with very long, slender sepals. A quicker calyx may be added using a rose calyx cutter if time won't allow a wired calyx. Cut five lengths of 28-gauge white wire. Work a ball of holly/ivy flowerpaste onto the wire, creating a long, tapered carrot shape. Place the shape against the non-stick board and flatten using the flat side of one of the double-sided veiners. If the shape looks distorted, simply trim into shape with a pair of scissors.

13 Place the flattened shape onto the foam pad or the palm of your hand, and soften and hollow out the length using the metal ball tool. Pinch the sepal from the base to the tip. Cut fine 'hairs' into the edge of the sepal using curved scissors. Repeat to make five sepals. I tend to leave one sepal without hairs – although remember there are some varieties of rose that have no hairs to their calyces at all.

14 Dust each sepal on the outer surface with a mixture of foliage and forest green. Add tinges of aubergine mixed with plum or ruby petal dust. Use the same brush used for the green mixture and dust lightly on the inner surface of each sepal with edelweiss petal dust. Lightly glaze the back of each sepal with edible spray varnish or half glaze.

15 Tape the five sepals to the base of the rose, positioning a sepal over a join. Add a ball of flowerpaste for the ovary, and pinch and squeeze it into a neat shape. Some florists' roses have almost no ovary – they have been bred out to prolong the life of the cut flower. Dust and glaze to match the sepals.

Leaves

16 I don't often use rose leaves as foliage in bridal bouquets, however, they are essential for arrangements. Rose leaves on commercial florists' roses tend to grow in sets of three or five. I generally make one large, two medium and two small for each set. Roll out some holly/ivy flowerpaste, leaving a thick ridge for the wire. Cut out the leaves using the rose leaf cutters. I like the shape of the black rose leaf set of cutters, however, these do not allow you to roll the paste too thickly as they are shallow and the paste often sticks to them. You just need to ignore this and carry on working. Insert a 30-, 28- or 26-gauge white wire moistened with fresh egg white into the leaf, depending on its size. I usually insert the wire about half way into the ridge.

17 Soften the edge of the leaf and vein using the large briar rose leaf veiner. Pinch from behind the leaf to accentuate the central vein and give more movement to the leaf. Repeat to make leaves of various sizes. Tape over a little of each wire stem with quarter-width nile green floristry tape. Tape the leaves into sets of three or five, starting with the largest leaf and two medium-size leaves, one on either side. Finally, add the two smaller leaves at the base.

18 Dust the edges with aubergine and plum or ruby petal dusts mixed together. Use this colour on the upper stems too. Dust the upper surface of the leaf in layers lightly with forest green and more heavily with foliage and vine green. Dust the backs with edelweiss using the brush used for the greens. Spray with edible spray varnish.

Note: the dark red roses on p 72–73 and 98–99 were made using ruby coloured flowerpaste and then dusted heavily with aubergine, plum and black magic petal dusts. The roses on p 102–105 were dusted with a mixture of plum, African violet and white petal dusts.

Parrot tulip

Tulips (*Tulipa*) start to make a re-appearance in florists' shops during the late autumn, early winter period. It is always a joy to see them again, especially my favourite multicoloured parrot tulips, known as parakeet tulips in Holland. The colour range is vast, from pure white tinged with green to many more flamboyant colour combinations. I love the red and green forms, especially at Christmastime, as their colour scheme fits in perfectly with the season. Parrot tulips are easier to make than the more formal straight-petalled varieties as more movement can be created and the colour streaks help create a more pleasing result.

Materials

- White, pale green and mid-green flowerpaste
- 33-, 26-, 24-, 22- and 18-gauge white wires
- Fresh egg white
- Edelweiss, vine, aubergine, plum, ruby, moss, foliage, daffodil, sunflower and forest petal dusts
- Isopropyl alcohol
- Edible spray varnish (Fabilo)
- Nile green floristry tape

Equipment

- Fine angled tweezers
- Plain-edge cutting wheel (PME)
- Dusting brushes
- Wire cutters
- Large tulip leaf veiner (SKGI)
- Fine scissors
- Fine paintbrushes
- Non-stick rolling pin
- Parrot tulip petal cutter (Cc) or template on p 108
- Scalpel
- Non-stick board
- Dresden tool (PME)
- Foam pad
- Large, medium and small metal ball tools
- Scissors
- Kitchen paper
- Fine-nose pliers

Pistil

1 Form a ball of well-kneaded pale green flowerpaste. Moisten the end of a 22-gauge white wire with fresh egg white and insert it into the shape. Work the flowerpaste onto the wire to form a sausage shape. Pinch off any excess as you work. The length of the pistil does vary between varieties – I try not to make it too large as it can be rather heavy looking in an open flower. I usually make it just under 2.5 cm (1 in) in length.

2 Flatten the tip of the pistil with your finger to form a sort of a 'nail' shape. Next, use fine angled tweezers to pinch the pistil into three sections from the side of the shape. Use your finger and thumb to pinch and pull out each section a little from the top to create a more defined realistic shape; having said that, some of the double parrot tulips have very deformed fringed centres. Mark a few lines onto each section using the scalpel or plain-edge cutting wheel. Allow to dry before dusting gently with a light mixture of edelweiss and vine petal dusts. Keep this light green mixture to dust the filaments later on.

Stamens

3 There are usually six stamens at the centre of the tulip, however, if the flower is double or semi-double in form, then there can be more stamens present too. Cut six short lengths of 33-gauge white wire. Attach a small ball of white flowerpaste onto the end of the wire and blend it firmly to create the filament shape: broad at the base and much finer at the tip. Next, flatten it using your thumb or the flat side of the large tulip leaf veiner. Trim the sides with fine scissors if the shape has altered too much. Repeat to make the six (or more) filaments required. Leave to dry if time allows before carrying on to the next step of adding the anther.

4 Attach a small cone shape of white flowerpaste to the tip of each filament. Blend it onto the existing paste and then flatten the anthers slightly. Mark a line down each side of the anthers using the plain-edge cutting wheel.

5 Dust the filaments with the same light edelweiss/vine mixture used for the pistil. The anthers can be cream, yellow or aubergine/brown in colour – I prefer the darker anthers as they create a more dramatic effect. Mix together aubergine petal dust with isopropyl alcohol and paint the anther of each stamen using a fine paintbrush. Allow to dry and then spray very lightly with edible spray varnish – this is to stop the colour coming off and marking the petals as you assemble the flower. Tape the six stamens around the pistil using half-width nile green floristry tape. Set aside until later.

Petals

6 I usually make six petals for each flower, but remember there are semi-double and double forms too. Using the non-stick rolling pin, roll out some well-kneaded white flowerpaste, leaving a thicker ridge at the centre for the wire. It is important that the paste is not too thin as a little fleshiness helps when texturing and veining the petals.

7 Cut out the petal shape using the parrot tulip petal cutter or use a scalpel to cut out the template on p 108. Insert a 26- or 24-gauge white wire moistened with fresh egg white into the thick ridge of the teal so that it supports about a third to half the length of the petal. The gauge of the wire will depend on the size of petal you are making. Here I have used a 26-gauge wire. Support the thick ridge firmly between your finger and thumb as you insert the wire.

8 Next, place the petal, ridge-side-up, against the non-stick board. Use the broad end of the Dresden tool to create the veins on the petal. Stroke and pull out the Dresden tool across the petal to create almost feather-like veining. This will also give extra shaping to the petal edges. Increase the pressure at the edges of the petal to create a frilled effect.

9 Use the fine end of the Dresden tool to cut into the edges of the petal and also to remove the odd slender 'S' shape from between the scallops of the petal shape. Some parrot tulips have very ragged edges, and remember that the petals can all vary in shape on one single flower.

10 Place the petal onto a firm foam pad or onto the palm of your hand and draw two lines onto the petal using the plain-edge cutting wheel. Turn it over and mark a gentle single line down the centre of the petal. Use a small- to medium-size ball tool to hollow out each section on the inside of the petal. Use a rolling action with the tool to create a more interesting shape to the petal. Pinch the petal from the base to the tip to accentuate the central vein and then dry for about 20 to 30 minutes before colouring and assembling the flower. Repeat to make six petals.

Colouring and assembly

11 Use plum and ruby petal dusts to create strong streaks of colour on both sides of each petal, remembering to leave room for any green, yellow or paler streaks as you work. A small flat brush is ideal for dusting these streaky effects. You will find the colour sticks a lot more easily to a freshly made petal as opposed to one that has been left to dry for hours. Use vine and then moss and foliage to create green streaks to the outer surface of each petal. Add the odd green tinge to the edges and the inside of the petals too. The markings can vary quite a bit between each petal on one flower. Add a few yellow tinges here and there if desired, using a mixture of daffodil and sunflower petal dusts.

12 Use half-width nile green floristry tape to assemble the flower. Tape three petals around the stamens to form the first layer, adding an 18-gauge white wire as you work to give extra length and support. Add the remaining three petals to sit over the gaps in the first three petals to form the outer layer. At this stage, if the petals are still pliable, curl and curve the shape to create a more realistic finish. Add extra petals if you are wanting to create a double or semi-double variety.

13 Extra detail can be added when the flower is fully assembled, adding extra splashes of colour or diluting some of the green petal dusts used with isopropyl alcohol and painting stronger detail onto the petals.

14 Thicken the stem and neaten it using half-width nile green floristry tape. Polish and smooth the stem using the sides of a pair of scissors. You may also use thin strips of kitchen paper wrapped around the stem prior to taping if you wish to achieve a fleshier finish. Dust the stem lightly with vine and foliage petal dusts.

15 Spray the stem lightly with edible spray varnish to set the colour. The flower may also be sprayed lightly, but take care not to glaze too heavily as this will result in a plastic-effect tulip. You might prefer to hold the flower once it has dried fully over a jet of steam from a just-boiled kettle or clothes' steamer to set the colour and give a little of the characteristic glossy finish that tulip petals have.

Bud

16 Use fine-nose pliers to bend a large open hook in the end of an 18-gauge white wire. Roll a ball of well-kneaded white flowerpaste and then form it into a cone shape. Moisten the hook with fresh egg white and insert it into the base of the bud. Work the base of the bud to secure it neatly to the wire. Divide the surface into three sections using a knife or the plain-edge cutting wheel. Add a couple of central lines to each section using the plain-edge cutting wheel. Leave to dry.

17 Roll out some white flowerpaste (no ridges this time!) and cut out three petals using the parrot tulip petal cutter or the template on p 108. Cut into each petal using the same cutter to create smaller cloud-shaped petals that are more suitable size-wise to fit the bud. Use the broad end of the Dresden tool to vein and cut into each petal as described for the petals of the flower in step 10.

18 Use the plain-edge cutting wheel to mark two veins onto one side of each petal. Use fresh egg white to attach the three petals over the deep divisions on the dried bud. Curl the top of each petal in slightly to form a triangular shaping as you attach them. Flick out the odd section of petal to create a little more interest in the bud shape. Dust and then paint detail as for the flower, adding more intense green markings to the smaller buds. Thicken the stems with fine strips of kitchen paper and tape over with full-width nile green floristry tape. Polish and dust the stems as for the flower.

Leaves

19 These are huge to make in flowerpaste. I tend to create some smaller leaves to use high on the tulip stem and then some larger leaves at the base. Even with real tulips I find their foliage can be very heavy to deal with when trying to put them in a vase. Roll out some mid-green well-kneaded flowerpaste, leaving a thick ridge down the centre for the wire. Use the large end of the plain-edge cutting wheel to cut out a freehand long strap-like leaf. Some tulips have broader leaves than others. Insert a 24- or 22-gauge white wire moistened with fresh egg white into about half the length of the leaf, supporting the thick ridge firmly between your finger and thumb as you feed in the wire.

20 Place the leaf onto a firm foam pad and soften the edges using the large metal ball tool. Texture the leaf using the large double-sided tulip leaf veiner, pressing firmly to create stronger veining, or use a packet of 33-gauge white wire pulled out of its wrapping to curve and press into the surface of the leaf, repeating the process a little straighter down the very centre of the leaf and then curving again on the edge. Repeat on the other side of the leaf too.

21 Pinch the leaf from the base to the tip to accentuate the central vein. Allow the leaf to firm up a little before dusting, then dust in layers: lightly at first with forest and then over-dust with foliage and edelweiss petal dusts. Add tinges of aubergine to the very edge if desired.

22 Tape onto the stem of the flower/bud, wrapping the base of the leaf around the stem if it is still pliable enough. Allow to dry a little more before steaming the leaves or spraying very lightly with edible spray varnish.

Kumquat

Kumquats are very closely related to the more familiar citrus family, however, they belong to the genus *Fortunella*. In fact, the flowers of the plant are very similar. These cute fruit are a great addition to any arrangement and bouquet, being both simple and quick to make.

Materials

- Pale vine green and holly/ivy flowerpaste
- 28-, 24- and 22-gauge white wires
- Fresh egg white
- Vine, tangerine, red, foliage and forest petal dusts
- Edible spray varnish
- Nile green floristry tape

Equipment

- Fine nutmeg grater
- Flat-headed cocktail stick
- Curved scissors
- Dusting brushes
- Rolling pin
- Simple leaf cutters (TT229–232)
- Fine textured rose leaf or fresh citrus leaf

Fruit

1 Roll a ball of well-kneaded pale vine green flowerpaste. Form the ball into a longer egg shape. Insert a hooked 24- or 22-gauge white wire moistened with fresh egg white into the slimmer end of the fruit. Pinch the flowerpaste to secure it firmly to the wire.

2 Texture the surface by rolling the fruit against a fine nutmeg grater. Use the flat end of a cocktail stick to create an indent at the tip of the fruit.

3 Snip a quick calyx into the base of the fruit using curved scissors.

4 Dust in layers depending on the ripeness you are trying to create with vine, tangerine and red petal dusts. Dust the calyx with a mixture of foliage and forest. Allow to dry, then spray with edible spray varnish.

Leaves

5 Roll out some holly/ivy flowerpaste, leaving a thick ridge for the wire. Cut out a leaf shape using the pointed end of one of the simple leaf cutters as the base of the leaf. You will need to use the four sizes of cutter to create a selection of foliage.

6 Insert a 28-gauge white wire moistened with fresh egg white into the thick ridge. Soften the edges and vein using the fine textured rose leaf or fresh citrus leaf. Pinch the central vein slightly.

7 Dust the leaves darker on the front than the back with foliage, vine and forest petal dusts. Allow to dry. Lightly glaze with edible spray varnish and tape over the foliage and fruit with quarter-width nile green floristry tape.

Gold hearts entangled and silver cotinus

Edible metallic spray paints create wonderful effects on flowers and foliage for Christmas designs. Here, I have used hearts entangled sprayed with edible gold spray paint, and also cotinus leaves sprayed with non-edible silver spray paint for a super bright finish.

Materials

- Pale green flowerpaste
- 33-, 30- and 28-gauge white wires
- Fresh egg white
- Nile green floristry tape
- Edible gold spray paint (APOC)
- Silver art spray paint or edible silver spray paint

Equipment

- Non-stick board
- Small ball tool
- Non-stick rolling pin
- Rose petal cutters (TT) or bougainvillea cutters (J)
- Poinsettia leaf veiner

Gold hearts entangled

1 Take a small ball of well-kneaded pale green flowerpaste and form it into a cone shape. Insert a 33- or 30-gauge white wire moistened with fresh egg white into the broad end of the cone and then place against the non-stick board. Use your fingers to press and squeeze the flowerpaste against the board to form a very naïve heart shape.

2 Next, hollow out the underside of the leaf using the small ball tool, working on both sides to encourage more of a heart shape. Pinch the leaf from behind to create a very gentle central vein. Repeat to make lots of leaves, pairing them as you work.

3 Tape two tiny leaves onto the end of a 28-gauge white wire using quarter-width nile green floristry tape. Continue to add the leaves in pairs down the stem, gradually increasing in size as you work. Add extra wire if needed to support the length. Spray in layers with edible gold spray paint. It is best to build up the gold in several layers to create a brighter finish.

Silver cotinus

1 Roll out some pale green flowerpaste, leaving a thick ridge for the wire. Cut out the leaf using either one of the rose petal cutters or bougainvillaea cutters. Insert a 28-gauge white wire into the thick ridge to support about half the length of the leaf.

2 Soften the edge and then place into a double-sided poinsettia leaf veiner. Pinch from the base to the tip to accentuate the central vein. Repeat to make leaves in graduating sizes. Allow to dry. Tape together into small groups. Spray with edible silver spray paint or in this case, for a super bright silver, use an art spray paint – these items are not intended to be eaten or placed directly onto the surface of a cake.

Mr Cool

Granulated and caster sugars combined with edible magic sparkles help to create a frosty finish to this adorable snowman that could melt many a cold heart! He was great fun to make, using just a set of biscuit cutters and a bit of imagination… and plenty of cut-out snowflakes too!

Materials

- 23 cm (9 in) oval fruitcake placed on a thin cake board of the same size
- 1 kg (2 lb 3 oz) white almond paste
- 1.5 kg (3 lb 5 oz) white sugarpaste
- 30 cm (12 in) oval cake drum
- White mimosa sugar balls
- Royal icing
- Broad pale blue metallic ribbon
- Non-toxic craft glue stick (Pritt)
- White and holly/ivy flowerpaste
- Bluegrass, black, tangerine, super red and holly/ivy paste food colours (optional), or ready-coloured flowerpaste in each of the colours listed
- White vegetable fat
- Granulated and caster sugars
- Clear alcohol (Cointreau or kirsch)
- Blue metallic dragées
- 28-gauge white wires
- Beige floristry tape
- Mug and saucer
- Cocoa butter, grated
- Bluegrass, black, tangerine, white, gentian, ruby and foliage petal dusts
- White bridal satin
- Edible white magic sparkles

Equipment

- Non-stick board
- Non-stick rolling pin
- Set of round biscuit cutters
- Small ball tool
- Piping bags fitted with no.3 and no.1 piping tubes
- Plain-edge cutting wheel
- Small oval cutter
- Small holly leaf cutter (OP)
- Assorted paintbrushes
- Snowflake cutters (KB)

Preparation

1 Cover the cake and cake drum as described on p 14–15. Attach white mimosa sugar balls around the base of the cake, using royal icing to hold them in place. Secure a band of broad pale blue metallic ribbon to the cake drum's edge using non-toxic craft glue. Leave to dry for a few days before executing the snowman design.

2 Mix together 50/50 white flowerpaste with white sugarpaste to create a pliable modelling paste for the snowman's body. You will need to colour a small amount of this paste with bluegrass food colour to create the scarf. If the flowerpaste is too firm, add a small amount of white sugarpaste to each amount of coloured flowerpaste – this will make the colours lighter but each element of the design is painted with coloured cocoa butter at a later stage so this is not a huge problem. Alternatively, ready-coloured flowerpaste is commercially available, which is helpful when small amounts of coloured paste are required, as mixing coloured flowerpastes can be messy!

Snowman design

3 You will need to refer to the snowman template on p 109 to create the exact sizing. Lightly grease the non-stick board with white vegetable fat and wipe it off with kitchen paper. Roll out the white 50/50 modelling paste not too thinly. Sprinkle over the granulated and caster sugars and then re-roll gently to embed the sugar crystals into the paste. Cut out three discs using three sizes of biscuit cutters. Soften the edges using your fingers and thumbs and then attach to the cake using clear alcohol to create a head, body and base.

4 Use the small ball tool to create sockets for the eyes and use the larger end of the piping tube to create a smiley mouth shape. Next, embed three blue metallic dragées into the middle section to represent the buttons – you might need a little royal icing to hold them in place if the paste has already started to dry. Roll two small balls of white 50/50 modelling paste and attach into the eye sockets. Roll two small black balls of flowerpaste and attach to the eyes to represent the pupils.

5 To make the nose, form a slender carrot shape out of tangerine flowerpaste and texture using the plain-edge cutting wheel. Moisten the broad end with clear alcohol and attach to the snowman's face. You might need to place a small piece of sponge or cotton wool under the tip of the nose to support it until it is firm enough to hold its own weight.

6 Colour some flowerpaste with bluegrass food colour. Roll out the paste fairly thinly onto the non-stick board. Use the plain-edge cutting wheel to cut out three short lengths to create the scarf. Create a fringe effect at the end of two of the longer sections using the plain-edge cutting wheel. Attach the scarf to the snowman's neck, starting with the two trailing fringed sections and then overlaying the shorter section. Give the scarf trails a bit of movement and flick the fringed sections a little too. Roll out some black flowerpaste not too thinly and cut out an oval shape using the small oval cutter to create the brim of the top hat. Soften the edge using your fingers and thumbs and attach to the snowman's head. Next, form the main body of the hat starting with a short sausage shape of black flowerpaste, flattening the edges and creating a slight curve to the shape as you work. Secure to the cake to complete the hat shape. Use the plain-edge cutting wheel to mark a band across the base of the hat.

7 Roll out a small amount of holly/ivy flowerpaste and cut out two tiny holly leaves using the small holly leaf cutter. Soften the edges and attach to the band on the hat. Add tiny rolled balls of red flowerpaste to represent the berries.

8 To create the twiggy arms, tape over two short lengths of 28-gauge white wire with beige floristry tape. Twist shorter lengths of tape back onto itself and add at intervals down the wire to create a twig-like effect. Carefully tuck the twigs underneath the main body section, taking care not to insert them into the cake itself. These items must be removed before the cake is cut.

9 To complete the design, melt some grated cocoa butter onto a dish above a mug filled with just-boiled water. Mix the various petal dusts in turn into the cocoa butter to create paints to add detail, shading and more depth to each section of the snowman using fine paintbrushes.

10 Roll out some white flowerpaste very finely and cut out a series of snowflakes in varying sizes using the snowflake cutters. Allow to dry a little before attaching to the cake with small dots of piped royal icing. Pipe a few swirls of royal icing at the base of the snowman using a bag fitted with a no.3 piping tube. Use a slightly damp paintbrush to brush and soften the piped swirls to give more of a snow-like finish.

11 Add detail spots to the snowflakes using melted cocoa butter mixed with white, bluegrass and a touch of gentian petal dust. Brush over the flakes with white bridal satin and then sprinkle some edible white magic sparkles over the snowman and the snowflakes to complete the design.

White Christmas

Elegant white Christmas roses provide a very peaceful quality to this beautiful Christmas cake. The composition is completed with the addition of edible silver leaf snowflakes!

Materials

- 15 cm (6 in) oval fruitcake placed on a thin cake board of the same size
- 350 g (12 oz) white almond paste
- 450 g (1 lb) white sugarpaste
- 25 cm (10 in) oval cake drum
- Fine green satin ribbon
- Royal icing
- Broad green velvet ribbon
- Non-toxic glue stick (Pritt)
- Edible silver leaf-covered flowerpaste
- Nile green floristry tape
- Food-grade plastic posy pick

Equipment

- Snowflake cutters (KB)

Flowers

- 4 Christmas roses, plus buds and foliage (p 20–23)
- 3 stems of snowberries (p 25)

Preparation

1 Cover the cake and cake drum as described on p 14–15. Attach a band of fine green satin ribbon around the base of the cake, using a small dab of royal icing or softened sugarpaste to hold it in place. Secure the broad green velvet ribbon to the cake drum's edge using non-toxic craft glue.

Silver snowflakes

2 Cut out several edible silver leaf-covered flowerpaste snowflake shapes (see p 17 for more information) using the snowflake cutters. These are very fine shapes so care must be taken when releasing the paste from them. There is a fine piece of metal supplied with these cutters that can be used to push the shape out of the cutter. Leave the shapes to dry for several hours.

3 Use small amounts of royal icing to secure the snowflakes onto the top and at the base of the cake.

Spray assembly

4 Group three Christmas rose flowers together and surround with two groups of foliage. Tape them together using half-width nile green floristry tape. Add two stems of snowberries and a Christmas rose bud to complete the display. Insert the handle of the spray into a food-grade plastic posy pick and then insert into the top of the cake. Tape together the remaining Christmas rose with one group of its foliage, plus a stem of snowberries. Place this small group at the base of the cake onto the cake drum.

Festive garland

A Christmas garland may be used as a table centrepiece, perhaps with the addition of candles at the centre or perhaps even a cake. Mostly, I use garlands around the home as wall decorations.

Materials

- Brown florist's twine (Oasis)
- Broad red ribbon

Flowers

- 2 trails of silver philodendron (p 38)
- 3 hellebores and 2 buds (Christmas rose p 20–23)
- 6 kumquats (p 54)
- 3 groups of ivy berries (p 29)
- 3 sprigs of yellow ilex berries (p 37)
- 5 trails of gold hearts entangled (p 55)
- 2 sprigs of holly (p 28)
- 7 silver tillandsia leaves (p 24)

Preparation

1 Twist and twine a few lengths of brown florist's twine back onto itself and then form into a garland shape, binding both ends together.

Assembly

2 Thread and twist a trailing stem of silver philodendron foliage around the garland on the right-hand side. Pull in the three coloured hellebores and their buds, twisting and hiding their stems into the garland as you work. Next, add the kumquats and a couple of groups of ivy berries.

3 Next, wrap a length of broad red ribbon around the garland, tucking in both ends to secure them. Continue adding more silver philodendron foliage, ivy berries and yellow ilex berries to fill out the remainder of the garland. Use the trails of gold hearts entangled to wrap and soften the edges of the display.

4 Tuck in a few sprigs of holly. Use the tillandsia leaves at intervals around the garland to curl and twist and add more interest in the arrangement. Finally, tie a large red bow at one side of the garland, leaving tails to trail.

Christmas wreath

A simple yet effective design that is an ideal first cake for a novice cake decorator or as a quick cake for the more experienced.

Materials

- 15 cm (6 in) round fruitcake placed on a thin cake board of the same size
- 350 g (12 oz) white almond paste
- 450 g (1 lb) white sugarpaste lightly coloured with bluegrass paste food colour
- 25 cm (10 in) round cake drum
- Very fine dark red satin ribbon
- Royal icing
- Broad dark red velvet ribbon
- Non-toxic glue stick (Pritt)
- Pale green, white and red flowerpaste
- Clear alcohol (Cointreau or kirsch)
- Small and large pearlized dragées
- Edible gold leaf-covered flowerpaste
- Mug and saucer
- Cocoa butter, grated
- Tangerine, edelweiss, white, sunflower, daffodil, foliage, forest, vine and ruby petal dusts

Equipment

- Non-stick rolling pin
- Non-stick board
- Fine leaf paper punch (L-Em)
- Small blossom cutter
- Silk veining tool
- Star cutter (TT)
- Small circle cutter
- Scalpel
- Ruler
- Assorted paintbrushes

Preparation

1 Cover the cake and cake drum as described on p 14–15. Attach a band of very fine dark red satin ribbon around the base of the cake, using a small dab of royal icing or softened sugarpaste to hold it in place. Tie three small bows using the same ribbon and attach at intervals around the base of the cake with dots of royal icing. Secure the broad dark red velvet ribbon to the cake drum's edge using non-toxic craft glue.

Garland design

2 Roll out some pale green flowerpaste thinly onto the non-stick board. Remove from the board and allow to dry for about 20 minutes. Feed the flowerpaste into the fine leaf paper punch and cut out eight sets of foliage. Using clear alcohol, attach three sets of foliage at intervals around the cake drum, and use the remaining leaves to create the basic outline of the wreath. Roll out some white flowerpaste thinly and cut out 12 blossom shapes using the small blossom cutter. Use the silk veining tool to vein and frill each petal. Attach the flowers in groups of three around the wreath, and a single flower onto each leaf section on the drum. Use a small dragée at the centre of each flower and attach larger dragées at intervals around the design – these will be painted to represent oranges. Cut out some stars and baubles from edible gold leaf-coated flowerpaste (see p 17 for more information) using the star and small circle cutters. Add them to the wreath and board design too.

3 Roll out some red flowerpaste thinly and cut narrow lengths of sugar ribbon using the scalpel and ruler. Cut two short 'tails' and remove a 'V' shape at the end of each. Attach at the base of the wreath using a dot of royal icing. Take another length of ribbon and bring the ends to the centre to form two loops. Cut and wrap a short piece of ribbon at the centre of the loops. Attach on top of the tails. Leave to dry.

4 Melt some grated cocoa butter onto a dish above a mug filled with just-boiled water. Mix the various petal dusts with the cocoa butter to create paints. Use tangerine and edelweiss to paint the large dragées to represent oranges. The smaller dragée flower centres are coloured with white, sunflower and daffodil. Use a mixture of foliage and forest to paint in the holly leaves and add a touch of vine green to paint in the detail on the cut-out fine leaves. Finally, add ruby to paint in the holly berries and add depth to the ribbon loop.

Silver lining

This silver tangled wire container creates a perfect base for a silver, white and green arrangement that looks great as a Christmas decoration for the home. Curls of silver aluminium, tangled balls of crimped florist's wire and a set of fine white festive lights help to extend and give character to this arrangement.

Materials

- Silver tangled wire container
- Florist's dry foam or staysoft
- 20-gauge white wires
- Nile green floristry tape
- Aluminium florist's wire
- Silver crimped florist's wire
- Fine LED white festive/fairy lights

Equipment

- Large scissors or wire cutters
- Fine-nose pliers

Flowers

- 2 trails of silver philodendron (p 38)
- 1 white poinsettia (p 40–43)
- 2 groups of silver tillandsia leaves (p 24)
- 3 groups of silver cotinus (p 55)

Preparation

1 Fill the silver wire container with a block of florist's dry foam or staysoft. Add length and strength to any of the elements by taping them onto 20-gauge white wire with half-width nile green floristry tape.

Assembly

2 Curve the two stems of the silver philodendron foliage and insert them into the staysoft to form a reversed 'S' shape. Use the single white poinsettia at the centre of the arrangement.

3 Cut a few lengths of aluminium florist's wire using large scissors or wire cutters. Use fine-nose pliers to curl and bend one end of each length. Insert into the arrangement, bending and curving the wires to define the shape of the arrangement and add interest.

4 Use the groups of silver tillandsia foliage to fill in the large gaps around the poinsettia and then finally add the silver cotinus foliage to soften the edges of the display.

5 Use silver crimped florist's wire to form tangled balls in varying sizes. Hang these from the aluminium wires and foliage stems. Finally, tangle a set of festive white lights around the base of the arrangement, along with a few extra tangled silver wire balls.

Candlelight

I bought this twisted silver candlestick to use on my table for Christmas lunch but I foolishly left it behind at the photographic studio on the first day of photography! Christmas is a bit of a blur at the moment and I now can't remember what I used instead as a centrepiece. Anyway, this is what I had actually planned to use – minus the green candles which belong to Sue Atkinson, the photographer.

Materials

- Nile green floristry tape
- Silver braid
- Green beaded wire
- 1 twisted silver candleholder
- Silver paper-covered wire
- 2 slender green candles

Equipment

Wire cutters or large scissors

Flowers

- 2 green hippeastrum (p 30–31)
- 1 dark red rose (p 46–49)
- 3 trails of ivy (p 29)
- 3 groups of silver cotinus (p 55)
- 3 sprigs of red ilex berries (p 37)

1 Tape the two green hippeastrum flowers onto either side of the large red rose using half-width nile green floristry tape. Trim off any excess wires or length using wire cutters or a large pair of scissors.

2 Add the trails of ivy to form an 'S'-shaped spray. Fill in the gaps using the silver cotinus foliage.

3 Use the three stems of ilex berries at intervals in the spray to brighten the edges. Finally curl and tangle lengths of silver braid and green beaded wire through the spray. Tie the spray onto the silver candle holder using silver paper-covered wire to secure it in place. Add the two green candles and check that the flowers are not too close to the flame before lighting the candles.

Christmas tree

The Christmas tree is one of the things I most look forward to during this festive time of year. This pretty tree is a combination of flowerpaste, rice paper, cocoa painting and gilded gold and silver decorations too.

Materials

- 25 cm (10 in) elliptical fruitcake
- 1.25 kg (2 lb 12 oz) white almond paste
- 1.25 kg (2 lb 12 oz) champagne-coloured sugarpaste
- 32 cm (13 in) elliptical Perspex board
- Broad gold metallic ribbon
- Royal icing
- White rice paper
- Edible silver and gold leaf-covered flowerpaste
- White flowerpaste
- Tangerine, foliage, bluegrass, myrtle, nutkin, ruby, African violet and teal, petal dusts
- Gooseberry paste food colour
- Clear alcohol (Cointreau or kirsch)
- Mug and saucer
- Cocoa butter
- Pink and turquoise metallic dragées

Equipment

- Jasmine leaf paper punch
- Snowflake paper punch
- Small dragonfly paper punch
- Small oak leaf paper punch
- Small and large star cutters (TT)
- Non-stick rolling pin
- Dusting brushes
- Small circle cutter
- Non-stick board
- Plain-edge cutting wheel
- Broad and fine paintbrushes
- Piping bag fitted with a no.1 piping tube

Preparation

1 Coat the cake as described on p 14–15. Transfer the cake to sit on top of the elliptical Perspex board. Attach a band of broad gold metallic ribbon around the base of the cake, using a dab of royal icing or softened sugarpaste to hold it in place. Leave to dry for several days.

2 Cut out lots of white rice paper leaves using the jasmine leaf paper punch. Cut out some edible silver leaf-covered flowerpaste snowflakes and dragonflies and some gold leaf-covered flowerpaste oak leaves (see p 17 for more information). Use the small star and a large star cutters to cut out gold stars. Roll out some white flowerpaste thinly and dust with tangerine petal dust. Use the small circle cutter to cut out orange shapes. Set aside.

Tree design and assembly

3 Mix together ¾ white sugarpaste with ¼ white flowerpaste and colour with gooseberry paste food colour. Roll out the paste onto the non-stick board and cut out the tree shape using the template on p 110 and a plain-edge cutting wheel. Lift and moisten the back of the tree with clear alcohol and attach to the top of the cake.

4 Melt some grated cocoa butter onto a dish above a mug filled with just-boiled water. Mix in foliage, bluegrass and myrtle petal dusts together. Use a broad paintbrush to apply the colour to the tree, forming a sweeping movement to create a tree-like texture. Mix another amount of melted cocoa butter with nutkin and myrtle petal dusts to paint in the tree trunk. Add darker finer detail lines if desired.

5 Apply melted cocoa butter to the back of each jasmine leaf and attach onto the tree in graduating sizes. Add extra smaller leaves to fill spaces. Be careful not to get the rice paper too wet as this will dissolve it. Leave to dry, then paint with the melted green paint to add detail and shading to the leaves.

6 Using the piping bag, pipe a dot of royal icing onto the back of the silver/gold dragonflies, snowflakes, oak leaves and small stars, and attach each element onto the tree. Next, add the cut-out oranges and the pink and turquoise metallic dragées, using tiny amounts of royal icing to secure them in place. Use the filled piping bag to pipe a series of dotted white piped flower designs around the tree.

7 Finally, add a trailing vine from the base of the tree to the tip, using the melted green cocoa butter and a fine paintbrush. Add tiny painted leaves to the design and then mix up smaller amounts of cocoa butter with ruby and then African violet petal dust to add dotted painted flowers to the vine to complete the design.

Christmas star

This stunning two-tier cake would be wonderful as a centrepiece for a large Christmas celebration or even as a Christmas wedding cake. Red flowers and gold stars are a winning combination and the moment this cake was photographed we all knew it was destined to become the front cover of this book!

Materials

- 15 cm (6 in) and 23 cm (9 in) round fruitcakes placed on thin cake boards of the same size
- 1.4 kg (3 lb 2 oz) white almond paste
- 1.8 kg (4 lb) champagne-coloured sugarpaste
- 33 cm (13 in) round cake drum
- Fine red satin ribbon
- Royal icing
- Broad red velvet ribbon
- Non-toxic glue stick
- Edible gold leaf-covered flowerpaste
- Clear alcohol (Cointreau or kirsch)
- Mug and saucer
- Cocoa butter, grated
- Ruby, foliage and vine petal dusts

Equipment

- Straight-edged sugarpaste smoother
- Star cutters (TT114–117)
- Fine paintbrush

Flowers

- 2 red poinsettia (p 40–43)

Preparation

1 Cover the cakes and cake drum as described on p 14–15. Place the small cake on top of the large cake and blend the edge using the straight-edged sugarpaste smoother. Attach a fine band of red satin ribbon around the base of each cake, using a dab of royal icing or softened sugarpaste to hold it in place. Secure the broad red velvet ribbon to the cake drum's edge using non-toxic craft glue.

Gold star side design

2 Cut out several stars shapes in graduating sizes from edible gold leaf-coated flowerpaste (see p 17 for more information) using the star cutters. Attach them to the cakes using clear alcohol or a tiny amount of royal icing.

3 Next, melt some grated cocoa butter onto a dish above a mug filled with just-boiled water. Mix in some ruby petal dust to create a paint and carefully add detailed dotted curls to the cake around the gold stars. Repeat with a paint made from foliage and vine petal dusts mixed together to complete the side design.

4 Carefully rest one poinsettia on top of the top tier and position the second one at the base of the bottom tier.

Materials

- Green florist's staysoft
- Fine red florist's cane
- Fine green crimped wire
- 2 red tea light holders and tea lights

Equipment

- Wire cutters or large scissors
- Pewter plate (or similar)
- Fine-nose pliers
- Large silver candle

Flowers

- 3 red poinsettia (p 40–43)
- 3 stems of scarlet plume (p 44–45)
- 7 twigs of red ilex berries (p 37)
- 5 maranta leaves (p 39)
- 5 dried lotus pods (p 36)

Christmas candles

I love using candles in floral arrangements, and Christmas allows me to use them with complete abandon. Here, a festive display of red, green and silver has been created as a beautiful table decoration.

Preparation

1 Place a ball of green florist's staysoft onto the side of the pewter plate, leaving enough space for the candle. Press the paste firmly against the plate to make sure it is well secured.

Assembly

2 Using fine-nose pliers, bend a hook in the end of each poinsettia stem and insert into the staysoft to create a focal area. Use the largest, most attractive flower at the centre. Next, add the three trailing stems of scarlet plume to add height and width and to soften the edges of the display. Add the twigs of red ilex berries, following the lines created by the scarlet plume, and use smaller sprigs to fill in other areas.

3 Use the maranta foliage to add interest and to fill in the larger spaces in the display. Add the dried lotus pods evenly throughout the arrangement to provide a more rustic edge.

4 Cut several varying short lengths of fine red florist's cane. Tie them to a length of fine green crimped wire, binding them as you add each one. Trail this line of red canes throughout the display to add another decorative element to the design. Finally, add the silver candle and two red tea light holders to complete this festive arrangement. Take extreme care when lighting the candles, making sure that none of the elements are too close to the flames.

Shining star

A berry-studded garland surrounds this small red star cake. The abstract snowflake decoration is a very simple and yet eye-catching way of decorating a Christmas cake.

Materials

- 15 cm (6 in) star-shaped fruitcake placed on a thin cake board of the same size
- 500 g (1 lb 2 oz) white almond paste
- 500 g (1 lb 2 oz) red sugarpaste
- White flowerpaste
- White rice paper
- Royal icing
- 5 dried star anise

Equipment

- Non-stick rolling pin
- Non-stick board
- Fine leaf paper punch
- Snowflake paper punches
- Piping bag fitted with a no.1 piping tube
- 20 cm (8 in) florist's twig garland
- Red crimped florist's wire

Flowers

- 3 trails of ivy (p 29)
- 15 stems of ilex berries (p 37)
- 3 groups of ivy berries (p 29)
- 9 Japanese clerodendron berries (p 33)

Preparation

1 Cover the cake as described on p 14–15. Pay attention to each point of the star as you coat the cake to keep cracking to a minimum. Allow to dry for a couple of days.

Decoration

2 Roll out some well-kneaded white flowerpaste thinly, release from the non-stick board and leave to dry for about 10 to 20 minutes. When the flowerpaste is firm enough and feeling more like paper in texture, slide it into the fine leaf paper punch. Cut out five sets of leaves. Cut out one large snowflake shape for the centre of the cake. Use rice paper or more dried flowerpaste to cut out five smaller snowflakes using the smaller snowflake paper punch.

3 Attach the larger snowflake at the centre of the cake using fine dots of piped royal icing. Secure the leaves to each of the five points of the star and then attach the five small rice paper snowflakes in between each of the points.

Assembly

4 Place the cake onto of the florist's twig garland. Thread and trail the ivy stems into and around the garland to frame the cake. Thread the ilex berries in groups around the garland with the odd stray stem to break up the space in between. Use the ivy berries and Japanese clerodendron berries in the same way, alternating them to complete the display. Tie the red crimped florist's wire around the star anise and add at intervals around the garland.

Materials

- 18 cm (7 in) round fruitcake placed on a thin cake board of the same size
- 750 g (1 lb 10 oz) white almond paste
- 900 g (2 lb) champagne-coloured sugarpaste
- 25 cm (10 in) round cake drum
- Very broad red satin ribbon
- Royal icing
- Broad green satin ribbon
- Non-toxic craft glue stick (Pritt)
- Decorative box to act as a base
- Nile green floristry tape
- Red and gold paper-covered decorative wires
- Food-grade plastic posy pick

Equipment

- Wire cutters
- Fine-nose pliers

Flowers

- 7 trails of gold hearts entangled (p 55)
- 2 green hippeastrum (p 30–31)
- 1 parrot tulip and 1 bud, plus foliage (p 50–53)
- 5 maranta leaves (p 39)
- 25 Japanese clerodendron berries (p 33)
- 3 stems of ivy berries (p 29)
- 3 stems of ivy (p 29)

Celebration

An unusual floral combination using the familiar colours of Christmas. Green hippeastrum as the focal flowers are surrounded and completed with the addition of Japanese clerodendron berries, red parrot tulips and trails of gold hearts entangled foliage.

Preparation

1 Cover the cake and cake drum as described on p 14–15. Transfer the cake onto the drum. Attach a band of very broad red satin ribbon around the base of the cake, using a dab of royal icing or softened sugarpaste to hold it in place. Secure a band of broad green satin ribbon to the cake drum's edge using non-toxic craft glue.

2 Place the cake onto a base to elevate it – here I have used a star-shaped box. Add trails of gold hearts entangled around the base of the cake board. Next, assemble the bouquet: tape together the hippeastrum and parrot tulip using half-width nile green floristry tape to form the focal point of the bouquet. Surround the flowers with the maranta leaves, Japanese clerodendron berries and ivy berries. Next, add loops of red and gold paper-covered wires, as well as some trails of wire too. Use the gold hearts entangled foliage and trails of ivy to soften and trail around the edges of the bouquet. Add and tape in a few groups of the clerodendron berries to the trails of paper-covered wires.

3 Insert the posy pick into the top of the cake and then insert the handle of the bouquet to hold it in place. Use fine-nose pliers to reshape any of the floral elements that need adjusting to create a more relaxed display.

Materials

- 15 cm (6 in) round fruitcake placed on a thin cake board of the same size
- 500 g (1 lb 2 oz) white almond paste
- 500 g (1 lb 2 oz) champagne sugarpaste
- Decorative gold square plate
- Florist's hessian banding
- 3 gold candles, plus holders
- Nile green floristry tape
- Food-grade plastic posy pick
- 3 dried orange and 3 dried lime slices
- 3 cinnamon sticks
- 5 sprigs of fresh rosemary
- 5 nutmeg and mace
- 5 star anise
- Red crimped florist's wire

Equipment

- Fine-nose pliers

Flowers

- 3 kumquats (p 54)
- 5 larch cones, plus twigs (p 26)
- 5 sprigs of yellow ilex berries (p 37)

Spiced delights

This is an effective way to use a combination of sugar flowers with fresh herbs and spices to create a last-minute Christmas cake. I have to admit that my own Christmas cake often takes this form as time is always so tight! Why not cheat a little!

Preparation

1 Cover the cake as described on p 14–15 Allow to dry for a few days.

Assembly

2 Place the cake on top of the gold square plate. Twist and wrap a length of florist's hessian banding around the base of the cake, tucking in both ends underneath the cake at the back.

3 Insert three gold candles supported by their holders into the top of the cake. Use half-width nile green floristry tape to tape together the kumquats, four of the larch cones and two sprigs of yellow ilex berries. Insert the handle of the spray into the posy pick and insert the posy pick into the cake. Carefully position the orange and lime slices underneath and behind the spray to fill in around the sugar flowers. Add the cinnamon sticks, fresh rosemary sprigs, nutmeg with mace and star anise wrapped with red crimped florist's wire to complete the top decoration. Use the remaining items around the base of the cake, placing them around the twisted hessian banding. Be very careful not to place elements of the design too close to the candles when they are lit.

Bright star

A star made from twigs forms an unusual framework and initial inspiration for this beautiful bouquet of Christmas roses, snowberries, tillandsia and silver philodendron leaves.

Materials

- 22-gauge white wires
- Nile green floristry tape
- Green florist's twine
- 1 florist's twig star
- Green and aqua florist's crimped wires

Equipment

- Fine-nose pliers
- Wire cutters/large scissors

Flowers

- 15 silver tillandsia leaves (p 24)
- 5 Christmas roses (p 20–23)
- 2 trails of silver philodendron (p 38)
- 9 stems of snowberries (p 25)

Preparation

1 First of all strengthen and lengthen any stems that need it by taping them onto 22-gauge white wires with half-width nile green floristry tape.

Assembly

2 Form a loose ball of green florist's twine and thread the ends through the centre of the twig star to form more bulk at the centre and also a handle at the back of the star/bouquet. Thread two stems of silver tillandsia foliage through the star and tape their stems onto the handle and the back using half-width nile green floristry tape. One stem should be slightly longer than the other. Curve them to form a reversed 'S' shape. Add one Christmas rose flower at the centre of the bouquet to form the focal point. This flower should stand slightly higher than all the others in the bouquet.

3 Continue to add the remaining Christmas roses so that they form a diagonal line through the display and fill up some of the space around the central flower. Add trails of silver philodendron leaves and green florist's twine to add length to the bouquet. Tape these in tightly and then curl the tips and curve the length to create more interesting shapes.

4 Add extra interest, adding the tillandsia foliage to snake through the whole length of the bouquet – these can be used to fill more space too. Finally, add the stems of snowberries dotted through the bouquet to fill in any remaining gaps. Use lengths of green and aqua florist's crimped wires to tangle and snake through the bouquet to complete the display. Use full-width nile green floristry tape to tape over the handle of the bouquet to neaten it.

Winter wedding

An elegant two-tier golden heart-shaped cake decorated with Christmas roses, snowberries and trails of silver tillandsia and philodendron leaves.

Materials

- 15 cm (6 in) heart-shaped dummy cake placed on a thin cake board of the same shape and size
- 23 cm (9 in) heart-shaped fruitcake placed on a thin cake board of the same shape and size
- 1 kg (2 lb 3 oz) white almond paste
- 1.8 kg (4 lb) white sugarpaste coloured with old gold food colour
- 33 cm (13 in) round cake drum
- Perspex tilting stand (Cc)
- Green satin ribbon
- Royal icing
- Broad green satin ribbon
- Non-toxic glue stick (Pritt)
- Tracing or greaseproof paper
- Sunflower, daffodil, plum, edelweiss, foliage, forest and myrtle petal dusts
- Clear alcohol (Cointreau or kirsch)
- Edible gold leaf-covered flowerpaste

Equipment

- Scriber or pen that has run dry
- Piping bag fitted with no.2 piping tube
- Assorted fine paintbrushes
- Star cutters (TT114–117)

Flowers

Bright star bouquet (p 86–87)

Preparation

It is best to use a polystyrene dummy cake for the top tier as the cake is tilted in this design. I have, in the past, used real fruitcakes tilted but I am always worried that they might slip off the tilting stand, so tend to advise the use a dummy cake instead. You can always make an extra cutting cake if needed.

1 Cover both the dummy cake and the fruitcake, as well as the cake drum as described on p 14–15 (but leave off the white almond paste covering on the dummy cake). Leave to dry for several days. Place the dummy cake onto the Perspex tilting stand using the pins supplied to hold it in place. Attach a band of green satin ribbon around the base of each cake, using a dab of royal icing or softened sugarpaste to hold it in place at the back. Secure the broad green satin ribbon to the cake drum's edge using non-toxic craft glue.

Brush embroidery side design

2 Trace the Winter wedding template on p 109 onto tracing or greaseproof paper and scribe it onto the top of the larger cake using a scriber or a pen that has run dry. Next, fill the piping bag with white royal icing. Pipe an outline around a petal in the design and brush the icing using a slightly dampened paintbrush to create the veined texture of the petal. Repeat with the rest of the flower. Add a series of piped dots at the centre of the flower to represent the stamens. Use the same process to fill in the leaf and bud sections.

4 Highlight the stamens of the flower using a fine paintbrush and a mixture of sunflower and daffodil petal dusts mixed with clear alcohol. Add a tinge of plum mixed with edelweiss and alcohol to catch the edges of the bud and flower. Use foliage, forest and edelweiss to paint in the leaves and trailing stems of the design. Use diluted myrtle petal dust to add spots to the leaves. Complete the design, adding tiny broken pieces of leftover edible silver leaf-covered flowerpaste (see p 17 for more information).

5 Assemble the bouquet (p 86–87). Insert the handle directly into the top of the dummy cake. Position the larger cake in front to allow the bouquet to trail over it. Complete the display, adding gold-coated flowerpaste stars to rest against the cake drum and trails of the bouquet.

Golden bell

A bell-shaped cake creates a novel, instant Christmassy feel to this eye-catching design. Using the floral elements to represent the handle of the bell add a quirky edge too!

Materials

- Fruitcake baked in a bell-shaped cake tin placed on a thin cake board the same size as the base's diameter (in this case 15 cm/6 in)
- 1 kg (2 lb 3 oz) white almond paste
- 1.5 kg (3 lb 5 oz) champagne-coloured sugarpaste
- 23 cm (9 in) round cake drum
- Fine and broad gold satin ribbon
- White royal icing
- Non-toxic glue stick (Pritt)
- Tracing or greaseproof paper
- Antique gold, bright gold, ruby, vine, foliage and white bridal satin petal dusts
- Clear alcohol (Cointreau or kirsch)
- Gold paper-covered wire
- Nile green floristry tape
- Food-grade plastic posy pick

Equipment

- Piping bag fitted with a no.1 piping tube
- Scriber or pen that has run dry
- Dusting brushes
- Fine paintbrush

Flowers

- 5 sprigs of yellow ilex berries (p 37)
- 3 sprigs of gold-sprayed ilex berries (p 37)
- 3 groups of silver tillandsia foliage (p 24)
- 3 stems of scarlet plume (p 44–45)
- 3 sprigs of holly (p 28)

1 Cover the cake and cake drum as describe on p 14–15. Leave to dry for a few days. Attach a band of fine gold satin ribbon around the base of the cake, using a dab of royal icing or softened sugarpaste to hold it in place at the back. Secure the broader gold satin ribbon to the cake drum's edge using non-toxic craft glue.

2 Half fill the piping bag with white royal icing. I piped the design freestyle onto the bell but you might prefer to trace the Golden bell template on p 110 onto tracing or greaseproof paper and then scribe it onto the cake using a scriber or a pen that has run dry. Allow to dry.

3 Once dry, dust the surface of the piped design with a mixture of antique gold and bright gold petal dusts. Next, highlight the design using a mixture of clear alcohol and the two gold powders to create a stronger line to the piped sections. Mix a little ruby petal dust with clear alcohol to highlight the berries and then a mixture of vine, foliage and white bridal satin to highlight the edge of the holly leaves.

4 Use three lengths of gold paper-covered wire plaited together to form a loop to represent the handle of the bell. Tape one stem of yellow ilex berries, one stem of gold-sprayed ilex berries, a group of silver tillandsia leaves, a sprig of holly and a stem of scarlet plume to the base of the loop using half-width nile green floristry tape. Curve the stems to follow the shape of the loop and insert into the posy pick, then insert the posy pick into the top of the bell. Re-arrange the elements to form a pleasing design. Use the remaining flowers, berries and foliage to form two trailing sprays to sit around the base of the cake. Rest the sprays in place to complete the design.

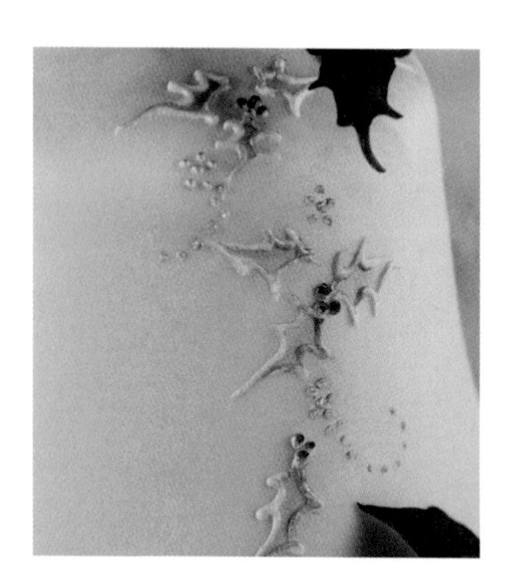

Winter stockings

It is not quite Christmas without hanging stockings in the hope that they will be filled with goodies. This cake combines holly, pine needles, stockings and snowflakes to create an instant festive design.

Materials

- 18 cm (7 in) round fruitcake placed on a thin cake board of the same size
- 750 g (1 lb 10 oz) white almond paste
- 900 g (2 lb) champagne-coloured sugarpaste
- 25 cm (10 in) round cake drum
- Green floral ribbon
- Thin gold ribbon
- Royal icing
- Broad red velvet ribbon
- Non-toxic craft glue stick (Pritt)
- White sugarpaste
- White, holly/ivy and red flowerpaste
- Clear alcohol (Cointreau or kirsch)
- Mug and saucer
- Cocoa butter, grated
- Foliage, white, woodland, vine, ruby and bluegrass petal dusts
- Edible gold leaf-covered flowerpaste
- Gold and antique gold petal dusts
- Edible gold stars

Equipment

- Non-stick rolling pin
- Stocking cutter (KB)
- Assorted fine paintbrushes
- Holly leaf cutters (OP)
- Dresden tool
- Plain-edge cutting wheel (PME)

Flowers

A few sprigs of holly (p 28)

Preparation

1 Cover the cake and cake drum as described on p 14–15. Leave to dry for a few days if time allows. Attach a band of green floral ribbon and a band of thin gold ribbon around the base of the cake, using a dab of royal icing or softened sugarpaste to secure them in place. Secure a band of broad red velvet ribbon to the cake drum's edge using non-toxic craft glue.

Stockings

2 Prepare a 50/50 mix of white sugarpaste and white flowerpaste to create a more pliable modelling paste. Roll out the paste not too thinly and cut out three stocking shapes using the stocking cutter. Soften the edges of each stocking using your fingers and thumbs. Place the stockings on top of the cake and carefully pad them out slightly using small amounts of white sugarpaste. Moisten the underside of the stockings using clear alcohol and secure them in place. Continue smoothing the edges down onto the cake to create a softer finish. Roll out some more of the mixed paste and cut out three bands using the cutter from the stocking set. Attach them to the top of each stocking using clear alcohol.

3 Melt some grated cocoa butter onto a dish above a mug filled with just-boiled water. Add foliage, white and woodland petal dusts to create a paint. Use a fine paintbrush to paint holly leaves above the stockings. Use foliage and vine mixed together to add fine pine needles to the edges of the display. Use ruby mixed with the melted cocoa butter to add berries. Leave to set.

4 Roll out some holly/ivy flowerpaste thinly and cut out several holly leaves using two small sizes of holly leaf cutters. Soften the edges and add a central vein to each leaf using the fine end of the Dresden tool. Curve and allow to firm up a little before attaching over the painted holly leaves using small dots of royal icing. Add tiny balls of red flowerpaste to represent berries at the centre of the holly leaves.

5 Add detail to the leaves using a foliage/woodland cocoa butter paint mixture. Use the ruby mixture to colour the berries. Replace the water in the mug to keep the mixture melted. Paint two red snowflakes in between the stockings and then mix up a small amount of bluegrass, foliage and white petal dusts together to paint two green snowflakes highlighted with red dots.

6 Paint the stockings using the various petal dusts, adding painted trees, stripes, dots and also gold highlights to create a festive feel using the gold and antique gold petal dusts). I have used tiny edible gold stars on the red stocking using dots of melted cocoa butter to hold them in place.

7 Roll out some red flowerpaste thinly to cut out lengths of red ribbons using the plain-edge cutting wheel. Attach the ribbons to the stockings, curling and looping them slightly to give movement and the impression that they are tied into the holly garland. Place a few sprigs of holly on the cake drum to complete the design.

Winter woodland

This unusual combination would be ideal for a grand cocktail party, wedding or birthday event during the Christmas period.

Materials

- 15 cm (6 in) and 23 cm (9 in) round fruitcakes placed on thin cake boards of the same size
- 1.4 kg (3 lb 2 oz) white almond paste
- 1.8 kg (4 lb) champagne-coloured sugarpaste
- 33 cm (13 in) round cake drum
- Broad gold organza ribbon
- Royal icing
- Broad dark red velvet ribbon
- Non-toxic glue stick (Pritt)
- Mug and saucer
- Cocoa butter, grated
- Nutkin, foliage and vine petal dusts
- Nile green floristry tape

Equipment

- Straight-edged sugarpaste smoother
- Fine paintbrushes
- Large food-grade plastic posy pick (W)

Flowers

- 1 full and 2 half dark red roses (p 46–49)
- 5 stems of winter jasmine (p 27)
- 3 trails of ivy (p 29)
- 2 larch twigs (p 26)
- 2 hippeastrum (p 30–31)
- 9 trails of gold hearts entangled (p 55)

Preparation

1 Cover the cakes and cake drum as described on p 14–15. Place the small cake on top of the large cake and blend the edge using the straight-edged sugarpaste smoother. Attach a band of broad gold organza ribbon around the base of each cake, using a dab of royal icing or softened sugarpaste to hold it in place. Secure the broad dark red velvet ribbon to the cake drum's edge using non-toxic craft glue.

Larch cone side design

2 Melt some grated cocoa butter onto a dish above a mug filled with just-boiled water. Mix in some nutkin petal dust to paint the scale formation of the larch cones onto the surface of the cake. Repeat to add the design at intervals over the surface of the cake and cake drum.

3 Next, paint in some larch twigs using the same paint mixture. Now make a paint from a mixture of foliage and vine petal dusts. Using a clean paintbrush, use this mixture to paint green needles and buds to the twigs. Allow the designs to dry and perhaps go back and add more detail using slightly darker paint mixtures.

4 Assemble the bouquet using the three dark red roses to create the focal area, taping them together with half-width nile green floristry tape. Add lengths of winter jasmine, ivy and larch twigs to extend and form the 'S' shape of the bouquet. Next, add the two hippeastrum flowers to frame the roses, and finally the lengths of gold hearts entangled to trail and soften the edges of the bouquet. Insert the posy pick into the top tier and then position the handle of the bouquet into it. Re-shape and relax the elements of the bouquet to create a wild woodland freestyle effect.

Glitter ball

Silver glitter balls and snowflakes combined with purple-tinged roses, snowberries and silver spray foliage create a wonderful Christmas party feel to this cake design. I have used glitter ball decorations wrapped with pink metallic wires to add to the tongue-in-cheek party vibe.

Materials

- 15 cm (6 in) round fruitcake placed on a thin cake board of the same size
- 350 g (12½ oz) white almond paste
- 450 g (1 lb) white sugarpaste
- 23 cm (9 in) round cake drum
- Fine purple satin ribbon
- Royal icing
- Broad purple satin ribbon
- Non-toxic glue stick (Pritt)
- Silver, metallic pink and pearl dragées
- Edible silver leaf-covered flowerpaste
- Large food-grade plastic posy pick
- Silver, purple and teal crimped fine florist's wires
- Silver glitter-coated paper snowflakes
- Mirror glitter ball decorations
- Purple and silver metallic florist's wires

Equipment

- Piping bag fitted with a no.1 piping tube
- Snowflake cutters (Kitbox)
- Scalpel
- Glass cake stand

Flowers

Glitter ball bouquet (p 102–103)

1 Cover the cake and cake drum as described on p 14–15. Attach a fine band of purple satin ribbon around the base of the cake, using a dab of royal icing to hold it in place at the back. Secure the broad purple satin ribbon to the cake drum's edge using non-toxic craft glue.

2 Fill the piping bag with a small amount of white royal icing and then pipe small dots to secure the silver, pink and pearl dragées in groups of three dotted at intervals around the cake. Cut out several snowflake shapes out of edible silver leaf-covered flowerpaste (see p 17 for more information) using the two sizes of snowflake cutter. Cut each snowflake into sections using the scalpel. Complete each decorative group with a section of snowflake.

3 Assemble the glitter ball bouquet. Insert the posy pick into the cake and then position the handle of the bouquet into it. Add extra trails of silver, purple and teal crimped florist's wires to trail in front of the cake. Add a few extra silver glitter-coated paper snowflakes too. Place the cake on top of the glass cake stand. Complete the display with extra mirror glitter balls tangled with purple and silver metallic florist's wires to tumble around the cake display.

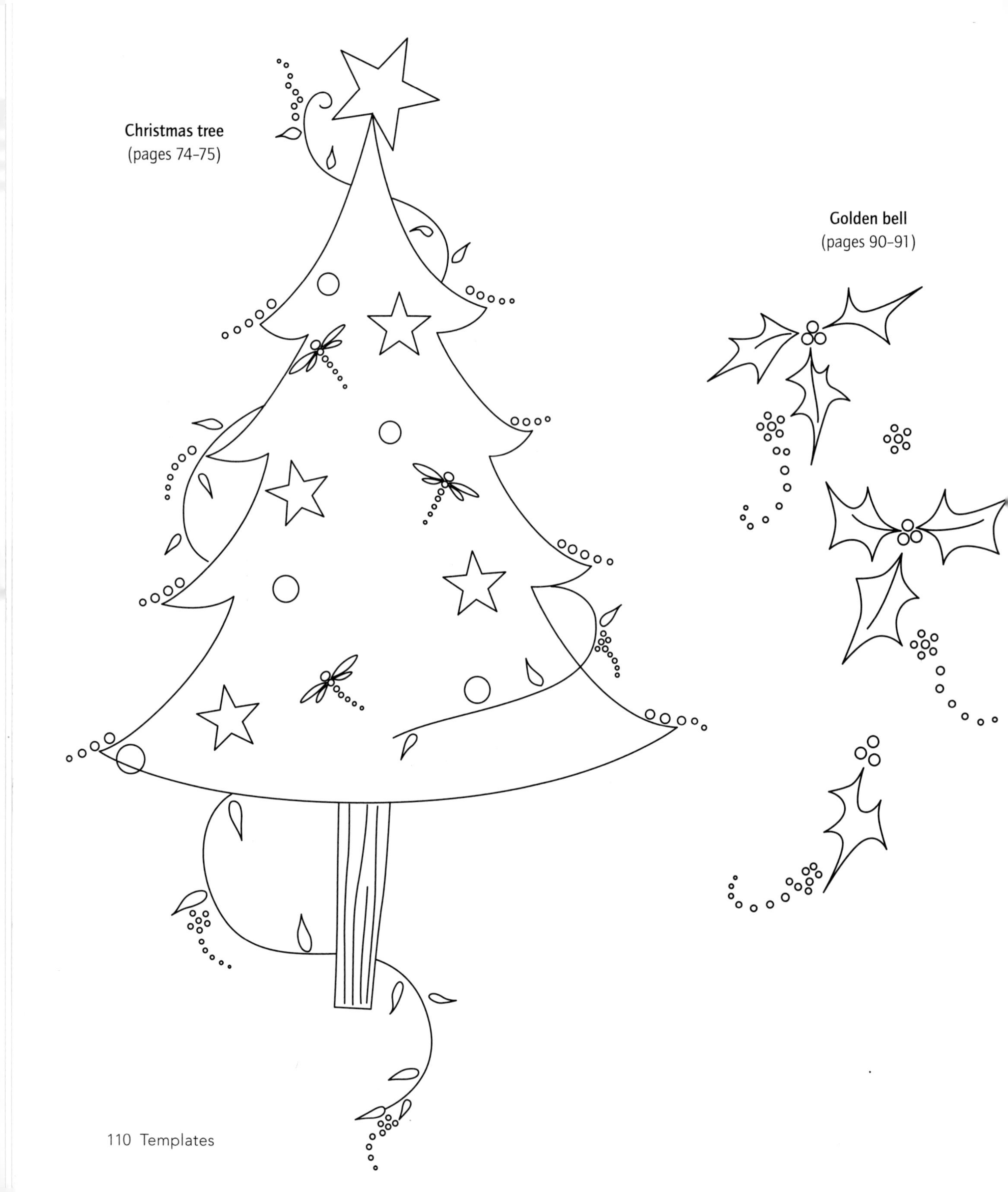
Christmas tree
(pages 74–75)
Golden bell
(pages 90–91)

SUPPLIERS

A Piece of Cake (APOC)
18 Upper High Street
Thame
Oxon OX9 3EX
www.apieceofcakethame.co.uk

AP cutters (AP)
Treelands
Hillside Road
Bleadon
Weston-super-Mare B24 OAA

Aldaval Veiners (ALDV)
16 Chibburn Court
Widdrington
Morpeth
Northumberland NE61 5QT
+44 (0)1670 790 995

Cakes, Classes and Cutters
23 Princes Road
Brunton Park
Gosforth
Newcastle-upon-Tyne NE3 5TT
www.cakesclassesandcutters.co.uk

Celcakes and Celcrafts (CC)
Springfield House
Gate Helmsley
York YO4 1NF
www.celcrafts.co.uk

Celebrations
Unit 383 G
Jedburgh Court
Team Valley Trading Estate
Gateshead
Tyne and Wear NE11 0BQ
www.celebrations-teamvalley.co.uk

Culpitt Cake Art
Jubilee Industrial Estate
Ashington
Northumberland NE63 8UG
www.culpitt.com

Design-a-Cake
30/31 Phoenix Road
Crowther Industrial Estate
Washington
Tyne & Wear NE38 0AD
www.design-a-cake.co.uk

Guy, Paul & Co Ltd
(UK distributor for Jem cutters)
Unit 10 The Business Centre
Corinium Industrial estate
Raans Road
Amersham
Buckinghamshire HP6 6EB
www.guypaul.co.uk

Holly Products (HP)
Primrose Cottage
Church Walk
Norton in Hales
Shropshire TF9 4QX
www.hollyproducts.co.uk

Items for Sugarcraft
72 Godstone Road
Kenley
Surrey CR8 5AA
www.itemsforsugarcraft.co.uk

Kit Box Cutters (KB)
Unit 4, Neads Court
Knowles Road
Clevedon
North Somerset BS21 7XS
www.kitbox4sugarcraft.co.uk

Orchard Products (OP)
51 Hallyburton Road
Hove
East Sussex BN3 7GP
www.orchardproducts.co.uk

The British Sugarcraft Guild
for more information contact:
Wellington House
Messeter Place
Eltham
London SE9 5DP
www.bsguk.org

The Old Bakery
Kingston St Mary
Taunton
Somerset TA2 8HW
www.oldbakery.co.uk

Tinkertech Two (TT)
40 Langdon Road
Parkstone
Poole
Dorset BH14 9EH
+44 (0)1202 738 049

Squires Kitchen (SKGI)
Squires House
3 Waverley Lane
Farnham
Surrey GU9 8BB
www.squires-shop.com

AUSTRALIA
My Cake Delights
219 High Street
Preston 3072
Melbourne
www.mycakedelights.com

CONTACT THE AUTHOR
www.alandunnsugarcraft.com

Index